MEMORY OF A MINER

A True-Life Story from Harlan County's Heyday

Dr. Michael Ruth

ℬ Growth Resources
Knoxville, Tennessee

Second printing 2014

ISBN (print book): 978-0-9905514-0-9

ISBN (eBook): 978-0-9905514-1-6

Front cover photo – 31 tipple in Black Mountain, courtesy of Marilyn Whitehead. Used by permission. Back cover photo – looking down the tracks in 31 Camp toward tipple, courtesy of the National Archives. Used by permission.

Acknowledgments

It is essential that I thank the following people for their contributions to this book: First and foremost, thanks to Dad and Mother – to Dad for his willingness to share his story, and to allow me to share it with others, and to Mother for filling in the gaps and for her invaluable clarifications. Thanks to my wife, Susan, for her tireless assistance with this project. As is everything we do, this book was a joint effort. Thanks to Jonathan and Jennifer who read the manuscript and gave feedback that has made this a better book. To the numerous people in Harlan County who gave bits of information and assistance along the way, thank you. I am sorry that I am unable to mention all of you by name. I would, however, extend my sincerest appreciation to two of their number: Marilyn Whitehead, for permission to use the cover photo and the late Joe Asbury for his invaluable information.

For Dad, because it is his story.

For Mother, because she lived it as well.

For Jonathan and Jennifer, because it is their heritage.

For Susan, because they all are.

Contents

PART ONE
WASHBURN TO COXTON

PART TWO
COXTON TO BLACK MOUNTAIN

PART THREE
BLACK MOUNTAIN TO HARLAN

Preface

Though I have checked the facts as I could, I want to state at the outset that this book is an oral history, not an academic treatise or a formal history. Were that my intent, I would have taken a far different approach and written in a much different style. This book, as the title implies, consists of recollections and stories recalled from one miner's memory. Moreover, it contains memories recalled and put to paper some fifty-five years after their day. Except for those clearly described as yarns, all of the stories are alleged to be true. In some cases, I have omitted or changed the names when discretion suggested it, but not the stories. Any inaccuracies are due to the fact that decades have passed since the time covered in this book, and memories are imperfect.

The spelling of names poses a particular challenge. Apparently, this problem exists even in the present. A research trip I recently took with Mother (Dad had passed away by this time) drives this point home. The street sign turning into what used to be 31 Camp says *Brittons* Creek. The historic Baptist church just across the bridge as you turn in is *Brittians* Creek Baptist Church. A street sign off Rail Lane (the primary road in what used to be 31), spells a road that turns off it *Britians* Court – one word, three spellings, all within a couple hundred yards of each other! So, as I said, the spelling of names is tricky business. (My most recent trip back reveals that the three names have been harmonized to that of the Baptist church – "Brittians.") If you are reading this and the name of a relative or someone else you knew or loved is misspelled, I apologize.

(As an aside, Mother found it amusing that the main road through the community now has a name – Rail Street. She remarks, "The whole time we lived here, when the mines was booming, the road didn't even have a name as far as I know. Now there's no mining, they've even pulled the tracks up, and it's called Rail Street!")

Speaking of names, throughout this book I use the prevalent name from the old days - *Black Mountain*[1] - when speaking of this part of Harlan County, and not it's official name, *Kenvir*.[2] I rarely, if ever, heard Mother and Dad refer to the area as Kenvir, except when speaking of their mailing address back then (which was P.O. Box 47, Kenvir, KY). Because most of the stories I have heard my entire life were anchored in *Black Mountain*, it seems completely unnatural for me to refer to the area as *Kenvir*.

Throughout the book you will find a number of endnotes. To enhance your reading, I would suggest that you turn to each note as you come upon the corresponding number in the text. Very often, there is a great deal of material in the notes that elaborates on the passage at hand.

The telling of this tale is many years in the making. The idea for this project first came to me in the early 1990s. There were many recorded conversations with Mother and Dad, usually around their dinner table. There were several trips to Harlan County with them, so they could point out and describe places of significance to me.

This is a book about a miner, not mining. Beyond that subject's most obvious points, I know very little about mining and certainly have no experience in it. Ironically, I am, in some respects, the least likely of the children to write a book about this period of Dad's (and Mother's) life. Why? Because *my* Dad was never a miner. Let me explain.

My memories begin after Black Mountain, once our family had moved to Harlan. I had just turned three when we made that move. The Dad of my earliest memories was a delivery man for Wardrup's Meat Packing Company, in Harlan. So this is what I mean when I say my dad was never a miner. His mining years were behind him when my memories begin.

These stories are from a different time and era. That time, full of its own faults, had at least one crowning advantage. It was not awash in the puerile dogma of political correctness, as we are today, where censorship is practiced rampantly and spun as virtue. I have not censored the stories herein. Some of them are, happily, in no way PC. I would encourage the reader who comes upon a word, phrase, or story which offends them to take a deep breath, steel their resolve, and read that section quickly. The stories are short and will soon pass.

When Dad is speaking in these pages, I want the text to sound like him. For this reason, I have retained his diction and manner of speech when the words are directly his own. In fact, I recorded many hours of conversation with Dad (and Mother), and then meticulously transcribed those tapes to digital copy. The very words themselves are put down here precisely as Dad spoke them on the recordings. I want you to not only hear Dad's words, but to *hear* the man himself. It may take you a bit to get familiar with Dad's style of speaking but once you do, you will be hearing Dad. To give the reader a fuller experience of Dad as you hear him, I have included a picture of him (and Mother) near the age in which we worked on this project together, so that you might *see* him as well as hear him.

After reading a draft of this book, Mother said, "Man, this sounds just like Carl. That's the way he would always tell it. I can just hear him." That is precisely what I was after.

Figure 1. Mother and Dad at a family wedding in 1988, about five years before we began this project.

Introduction

The title of this book is intentionally ambiguous. Two meanings are implied. My first intention with the title is to establish that this book has as its primary source – the memory of a miner. Memory is the recall of personal experience, and that is what you will find in these pages – my dad's experiences as an old-school Harlan County miner for twenty-eight years. My interest, as the preface notes, is not to establish a proper history in any sense of the word. The second intent of the title is to convey the fact that I am writing this as a memorial to my father – "In Memoriam," as the phrase goes.

This tale is a visitation into one man's story. As such, it is the story of joy and sadness, success and failure, hardship and bounty, and gains and losses, on an intimate scale. It is the story of all that was uniquely his, and all that made him uniquely him.

Journalist and storyteller Ira Glass says, "Great stories happen to those who can tell them."[3] By that measure, Dad lived a cracker jack of a life in his mining years. Man, did he have stories to tell – and could he ever tell them!

I loved to have Dad tell me of his memories and adventures from the mining days. Over the years, I had him repeat them to me many times here and there. It's not that I forgot any of them. It's just that I so very much enjoyed *how* he told them. Dad's stories never failed to stir the emotions because of his skill in telling them. He was a raconteur of the first order. His stories were either incredibly funny or unbelievably weird, or heartbreakingly sad. His telling always matched the content and mood of the tale.

I know those years from Mother and Dad's life from the memories they have shared with me since...forever. These stories – the lore of my life – are rich and alive to me. And lore is important, for it is the vital loam from which so much of our life emerges. It is crucial that a family (a region, a nation, for that matter) keep its lore alive. There is no understanding a person, any person, without knowing that person's inherited story.

In conjunction with research for this book, I recently made another trip to Harlan County. Every time I return I see that, like the tide eroding a beach, time is erasing the physical evidence of so many of the stories you're going to read here. For example, the building which is absolutely central to the events of Chapter 6 is no longer there. The nearest thing to that spot now is a massive concrete pillar that supports the new Highway 421 built overhead.

The point is quickly approaching in which the lore of the old-school miner will exist only in the memory of a dwindling population of immediate relatives, itself rapidly disappearing, and in written records like this one. This is an incredibly sad fact. They deserve better.

PART ONE

WASHBURN TO COXTON

CHAPTER 1

To a Thing Born

Carl Ruth was a coal miner. After moving his family from Harlan to Knoxville, Tennessee (1965), he may have had a number of different jobs, but that's all they were. They were a way to provide for his family and, for Dad, that was the biggest part of being a man. He worked for a short while with a neighbor as a commercial fisherman. He was in residential construction for a bit after that and, finally, as a bead grinder in the business of laying natural gas pipelines.

These were jobs for Dad and he worked hard at them. As he did with everything he undertook, he gave them his best. But that's all they were – jobs. A means to an end. They were never his career and they never held his heart.

Dad's heart belonged to mining. That was his only and true career. The day he pulled out of mining, he moved out of his world. He left a lot of himself back in those Harlan County hills.

To his dying day Dad was ever ready to talk mining at any time. When TV news brought stories of a cave-in, explosion, or some other mining catastrophe, the old miner would watch intently, and often in tears. He'd stay with the story until its all-too-often tragic resolution. If you were observant, you could tell that during that time his mind was somewhere else. In heart and soul he was with those men and with their sick-worried and grieving families. "To me that's the saddest death there is," says Dad. Whether suddenly from a roof fall or slowly from being blocked off from breathable air, or violently from a coal dust or methane gas explosion, Dad reckoned a miner's dying on the job to be the most lamentable way to exit this world. He had seen enough of these deaths to have earned the right to his opinion.

Upon his retirement, Dad and Mother bought some property just outside of Knoxville. From Dad's perspective, their home lacked something. He decided he needed a basement. He didn't really need the basement, for he would soon build a grand outbuilding for storage and to work in – to "piddle," as he called it. But it wasn't enough. He needed to mine. The earth was calling to him in ways only an old miner could understand. So, with tools basic and familiar – pick and shovel – he took to the back-breaking work of digging. Dad was nearing his seventh decade on this earth while he was digging that basement, but no matter. He was in his world, in his place, and he was happy.

CHAPTER 2

A Brand Plucked from the Fire

Carl L. Ruth was born on July 30, 1916, in Washburn, Tennessee. Washburn is in Grainger County, the area of the verdant, rolling hills of East Tennessee, now so famous for its succulent tomatoes.

Even the beginning of Dad's life was more confounding than usual. I remember when I was quite young asking Dad what the "L." stood for in his name. "Aaah [his favorite expression, pronounced as the short a in "bat"] nothin' I don't reckon, honey. They always just said it was L."

The practice of giving a child a letter instead of a middle name was not that unusual around the time Dad was born. The story doesn't end there, however.

One early-summer day I drive the twenty minutes down to my parents' house to visit a bit. (This was the period in which I began to think about writing his story.) We get to talking about Dad's early years. Unable to remember certain key dates, Dad says abruptly, "Hey, wait a minute. I bet that stuff's in the old family Bible!" He gets up from his chair and heads down the hall to the bedroom. In a few minutes, he returns with a very old and use-worn black Bible. Dad hands the Bible to me. He is right. It is a trove of information.

One particular entry pops from the page for me, though. I begin to chuckle and get a bit energized. I know instantly that what I have discovered has the makings of one of those hilarious Dad moments. I loved those!

The entry in that old Bible for Dad's birth is not "Carl L. Ruth," as he thinks and as we have all been told. Rather, in that beautiful penmanship of a bygone age is written, "Carl L. E. Ruth."

"Dad, according to this, there's an 'E.' in your name." (This is going to get good, I'm thinking!)

"Well honey, I've always spelled it C-a-r-l, that's how it was told me. I never knowed they was an 'e' on the end."

By now I'm just flat out laughing. I always cherished those times with Dad.

"No, Dad," I begin to explain, "your name is written as Carl L. **E**. Ruth!"

"Well, [another common expression of Dad's, always accompanied by a "if that don't beat all" look on his face] that sounds about right," he says.

Now, Mother and I both are belly laughing.

"I've never heard that before," says Dad.

I rise from the couch, walk to Dad's chair, and show him.

"Boys, I'm tellin' you what's the truth, if that don't beat all!"

I'm laughing tears, Mother is close to that point, and now Dad's laughing – laughing and getting on a roll!

"I always knowed I didn't know much, but I thought at least I knowed my name!"

Mother: "You reckon that's right, Carl?"

Dad: "Well, surely to goodness it is, honey! Somebody wrote it in the family Bible!"

Mother asks, "Well, what do you reckon it stands for, honey?" [As any Southern reader will recognize, "honey" is just about a second name for everyone in the lower half of Appalachia.]

Dad answers through a chuckle, "I don't know, honey. I've never heard that. I don't have no idee what it stands for!"

Until his dying day, this mysterious matter of his name was the source of a good laugh between us. I would randomly say, "Dad, tell me again about that name of yours," or some such. He would typically reply, "What about that, buddy. Ain't that somethin'. You'd think a feller could at least get his name right!"

(Turns out the acorn didn't fall far from the tree in this matter of names. According to Dad:

> I never knowed for sure what Poppa's name was. I'd always heard it was George Orville Ruth but some of 'em said it was Gaius Orval. I'd hear some of 'em from time-to-time say that was his name. But I never knowed of nobody calling him by that in my whole life. So I'm like Poppa I reckon when it comes to my name!)

———————————

Though he would later be a miner himself, my Grandpa Ruth was a railroad man, early on. More specifically, he was a fireman. It is funny how word meanings change over time. In the old days of railroading, a fireman didn't put out fires, he started them and fed them! The fireman's job was to shovel coal in the boiler furnace, to keep the steam up. The steam propelled the train. (A perk of Grandpa's job was that the workers received passes which allowed them and their family members to ride free in the caboose.)

Like nearly everyone else in rural areas in the early 1900s, the Ruths grew and raised their own food. All manners of vegetables were farmed and they kept pigs, chickens, a couple of beeves, and a milk cow. Dad calls upon the family lore passed to him from parent and sibling to tell me about this time in his life. He was but a babe in arms.

One of these stories involves his oldest brother, Lawrence (only child at the time), and a very protective family pet. While Grandpa (George Orville) and Grandma (Etta Mae) were working the crops, they would make a pallet for little Lawrence nearby and place him on it. The family dog, a pit bull mix named Rex, was commanded to sit near Lawrence as protector. So committed to his charge was this four-legged guardian that the only person he would allow to come and get the child was the one who laid him on the pallet. Rex would not even allow other family members to pick Lawrence up!

"Man's best friend" was useful in other ways as well. If Grandpa wanted to retrieve a particular hog he would set Rex on the task. In Dad's words, "That dog would catch him, get him by the rooter [snout] and sling that hog down and flop him on his side." Rex would then hold the hog in place until Grandpa got there.

In the fall of 1916, a family crisis would push the family to Kentucky.

I was just a baby and they said Mother had just made me some clothes. They'd gathered the crops and everything in. Dad had stacked the flour and wheat. We had a closed-in back porch you see, and Dad had the season's grain ground and bagged and had it stacked up to the ceiling on that porch. They'd killed their meat for the comin' winter. Mother had canned all the vegetables and strung the shuck beans for dryin' and the porch was filled with all that food.

This is one of those endearing images known throughout the rural South as well as other bucolic areas of our country even today.

On a crisp late-fall night with the bite of an approaching mountain winter enveloping the hills, chaos erupts. The house is afire. Well, that doesn't rightly say it. The house is burning down! Grandma and Grandpa are scurrying frantically to wake and rouse all the kids. Amidst the shouting and turmoil, they flee the inferno.

Some months later the truth of that fire (until that time a mystery) came out. It happens that another man had wanted the house and land where Grandma, Grandpa, and their children lived. The man was angry that the property had not been sold to him instead and, in his covetous anger, he set fire to the house that cold night. The man, name unknown, confessed to the deed on his deathbed. His pathological pettiness nearly cost a family of eight their lives.

It did, in fact, cost them nearly all their earthly possessions. The only items salvaged were an old pedal-driven Singer sewing machine and "that old dresser we had that Sis [my Aunt Emma] had for a while. You remember that, honey?" Dad says to Mother. He continues, "There was a rose-like of a thing burned into it where it got so hot the quicksilver melted off the mirror and it looked like a big rose."

I said that all escaped the fire, but that is not entirely accurate. Dad, still an infant, did not escape. He was rescued. One of his parents, he no longer recalls from the story which, "Put me in a pillar slip [pillow case] and throwed, dropped me out the window. Some of 'em outside caught me. I don't remember now which one of 'em they said caught me. I used to know that. That's how I got out." Dad was rescued, in a very Biblical sense, "like a brand plucked from the fire."[4]

CHAPTER 3

The Boy is Key to the Man

To understand a man, you must understand the boy he was. (Which is why those in my profession, psychological counseling and psychotherapy, routinely say "Tell me about your childhood.")

Dad grew up the youngest[5] child in a family with one girl and a gaggle of boys. This meant that he was also the youngest boy. The position where there are older brothers, four in this case, can be a hard position to occupy.

Power is an interesting thing and what people do with it, even more so. There is a good chance that any memories you have from your childhood of being hurt (or hurting others) likely involve some abuse of power. Power comes in several forms. Some examples are: power of position (a parent, a boss, for example), power of popularity, power of wealth, power of intelligence, power of affluence, and the most basic of all – physical power. Power is a neutral force, meaning that it can be used positively or negatively. The positive use of power is what we call goodness. Evil is the negative use of power.

The powerlessness Dad felt[6] as the youngest – and therefore the weakest – brother contributed to his becoming an often angry and defensive young boy. Even into old age, that anger never fully left him. Dad's anger was like the bass line in a song. It was not always prominent, but it was there.

Many times I've heard Mother say, "Carl, why don't you pray about your temper?" As I write this and recall Dad's ever constant answer, I smile. I smile because, ironically, the question always made him mad! Dad's answer to her question never varied. "Honey, I've prayed about my temper my whole life. It don't do no good!" Even to his death it would be fair to say Dad never did really conquer his anger, though he did get much better at managing it.

Dad's journey turns from family stories told him to his own personal memory when he is five years old. From Washburn, Tennessee, the family moves to downtown Middlesboro, Kentucky, on 25th Street, as Dad recalls. (Middlesboro, originally Middlesborough, is named for the coal and iron city of Middlesbrough in England. Note some of the prominent street names in Middlesboro: Worcester, Manchester, Dorchester, Exeter, Gloucester - all English.) Dad remembers that Grandpa worked as a carpenter at that time. For a brief period, he supplemented his income by working as a sheriff's deputy in the capacity of jail guard.

Dad shares an interesting recollection from the time in which Grandpa was guarding the jail:

I remember when the Colson's and the Ball's got into it; they was a-feudin', and the law had some of 'em in jail there in Middlesboro. Dad had to guard them, there in the jailhouse. They was feuding between each other about somethin'. I don't recall what it was about. They was a mean bunch, I reckon. That's what I always heard. I know Dad was concerned they'd be trouble over them that was in jail.

Well might Grandpa have been concerned over this matter. The Colson-Ball feud actually spilled over into the Bell County Courthouse in Pineville, where George Colson was on trial for the murder of Ira Ball. It was an old-fashioned shootout which began in the office of the circuit court clerk and immediately spread to the corridors of the courthouse. One man was killed instantly and two others were expected to die on route to the hospital. Five men were arrested and transported to the Middlesboro jail where Grandpa was in charge of guarding the prisoners. The story even made it into the *New York Times*, no doubt reinforcing the stereotype already firmly in place about the wild behavior of "hillbillies."[7] Knowing the full details of this story, it is little wonder Grandpa was anxious about his duty as a jail guard at that time!

Primarily though, Grandpa worked as a carpenter. He built houses, furniture, just about anything that had to do with wood. He helped build one of the early theaters in downtown Middlesboro. Carpentry was a skill my Grandpa would put to use time and again in his life, even after he went on to mining. Dad learned a lot about woodworking and carpentry from Grandpa. Although he never worked at the trade professionally, Dad was an excellent carpenter.

Dad started in the first grade at Middlesboro Elementary. "I remember they had a cannon with cannonballs stacked up out front at the school, kindly like decoration, you know." As a first grader, the separation anxiety and insecurities sometimes seen in children of that age began to show.

> Ed and Chalk [older brothers, the two nearest Dad in age – Ed was the older of the two] would be a-goin' in front of me, you see, and I didn't want to go to school. They was a stove in the kitchen, a cook stove, that set across the corner caddy-cornered. I'd crawl back in the corner behind the cook stove, you see. I'd let them get down to the Coal Iron Bank building, I'd foller along behind 'em til they'd get down there and then when they'd turn the corner at the bank building, I'd turn and take back off for the house. And they'd have to come – they'd miss me and they'd have to come back and pull me out from behind the stove for I'd crawl back in there behind the stove.

Dad couldn't remember why he was so resistant to going to school. As we talked about this, Dad said something that struck me as quite pitiable.

"Why didn't you want to go to school?" I asked.

"I just didn't. I wanted to stay at home."

I continued, "Were you a Momma's boy growing up?"

"Nah, I wasn't. I wasn't nobody's boy, I don't believe."

There is a difference between *being* loved and *feeling* loved. I am sure that Grandpa and Grandma Ruth dearly loved their children – loved them and tended to their every need as best they could. Grandma especially sounds like the kind of person who could not have done otherwise. But for reasons unknown, even though he *was* loved, Dad didn't *feel* loved.

Dad recalls a poignant story from the Middlesboro days involving his brother Ervin (next to oldest) and Grandma. The year is 1923, and much of Europe is still crawling out of the devastation of WWI. Grandma is working in the kitchen when her son Ervin walks in to chat with her. He tells his mother he is going into town to have a pair of shoes repaired. Ervin is chewing gum and he asks Grandma if she wants "a cake of gum." She takes the piece of gum and drops it in her apron pocket. Ervin walks out of the house and down a few blocks to a familiar building in Middlesboro. His destination, however, is not as he has told his mother.

As it turns out, Ervin was not going to have his shoes repaired. He had, earlier and secretly, joined the Army. It would be months before Grandpa and Grandma Ruth saw their son again. Perhaps there were mitigating circumstances, but Uncle Ervin's approach to enlisting in the military always struck me as a terribly cruel one. I can't imagine what that was like for his parents.

That stick of gum? Grandma Ruth kept it. I suppose for her, it provided a meager connection to her now-departed son. Near the end of her life, Grandma passed that "cake" of gum on to my dad. A few years before his death, Dad passed it on to me. I still have it to this day – a 1923 stick of Clark's Teaberry gum.

From downtown Middlesboro, the family moved to the Columbia community of Bell County. This would turn out to be a critical juncture in Dad's story, for this is where coal mining enters the picture. The move from Middlesboro to Columbia happened because Grandpa obtained a mining job at the Hignite[8] mine there, not only for himself, but for the eldest son, Lawrence, as well. Dad was about eight years old at the time.

Dad's chief recollection from these years involves the evidently very common brotherly fights that took place between the three youngest children: Ed, Chalk, and Carl. (The oldest three siblings were adults and were not a factor in these childhood skirmishes.) With the remorse that comes with age Dad says "We wore our poor ol' blessed Mother out a-fightin' all the time."

Being the youngest and unable to match Ed and Chalk in physical power, the young Carl discovered that a rock was the great equalizer. Not only did it pack a wallop, it had the added benefit of meaning that you didn't have to be in reaching distance! Moreover, a rock provided several yards of head start, should running become the prudent option. The story of the three youngest Ruth boys was a familiar one to the mountains. They fought like cats and dogs among themselves, but pity the outsider who attacked one of them.

Dad was in the third grade now. He still had developed no love for school. This self-described "ol' country-looking boy," remembers how he and his brothers, Ed and Chalk, would cross the creek on rocks to get to school. "We carried our lunch together because we all three eat together. We carried it in an eight-pound lard bucket, or either a little four-pound lard bucket, if you carried it just for yourself."

One of the more memorable brotherly fights, this one a "whopper" as Dad puts it, was about to occur. In Dad's words:

Well, we was in the house and me and Chalk and Ed got in a fight. Poor ol' Mother had hung out a washin' that she had washed on a washboard. And she had hung it out on the clothesline that run from the house to a big oak tree out in the yard.

We got into it a-fightin' and we was a-fightin' around the potbellied stove in the livin' room and we turned the stove over. Soot went to flyin' everywhere! It went out the chimney and out the stove pipe and out the windows. The soot just covered the washin' that Mother had hung out, buddy. Poor ol' Mother had to do her washin' all over again, on her washboard by hand.

Here is another story that illustrates how the younger brothers often settled their differences. This one involves the three usual suspects but Dad and Chalk seem to have got the worst of this one.

Me and Chalk was rockin' each other and he stuck his head out from behind the boulder he was usin' for cover. Well, just about that time my rock caught him in the head! Chalk and Ed wouldn't let me go with 'em, you see. They was just goin' out to play but I was like you was Mike, the youngest [I am the youngest of four]. They didn't want to take me with 'em. Well, you didn't get nowhere with that with me! So, I'd just take up for myself. I know it brought blood, where I hit Chalk in the head with that rock. He went back down to the house and they patched him up. I know I got a good whippin'!

I remember another time, when Mother was settin' on the front porch sewin' on that ol' pedal Singer that they saved from that fire we was in in

Washburn, when I was a baby. Well, Ed and Chalk had got into it about somethin', we was all just young boys then. I'd always side with one of 'em when they was at it with each other 'cause I wasn't big enough to fight one of 'em by myself, you see. Whichever one I sided with, we'd pour it on the other one buddy! This time I sided with Chalk.

We was fightin' our way through the house and ended up in the kitchen. Ed was going to get out the kitchen door and I picked up a cane-bottom chair at the table there and whacked him across the back with it. I knocked him plumb out that back door buddy! It was just one of them typical kid fights. We was fine with each other in a little while. I loved it when I got to side with one of them two, 'cause being the youngest I was usually the odd man out. They didn't want to have to fool with me when they played and went places, you see.

Following a better mining job, Grandpa and family headed from the Columbia community to Shields, in Harlan County. (Shields is located about halfway between Evarts and Closplint.) Grandpa would shortly go to work there for the Pennsylvania, Virginia & Kentucky Coal Company, or PV&K Mines, as it was known.

Before that, however, Grandpa's carpentry skills would be put to use again. He was hired to build a new house for Tom Sharpe, the Sharpe of Cook & Sharpe Mining Company[9] (located in Lejunior, which is between Shields and Highsplint). Dad recalls, "Man, it was a big thing. It was a big, pretty frame house with a screened in back area. It was painted white."

In PV&K a school-related story stands out once again for Dad who is, at this point, about ten years old.

> We was gettin' water, drinkin' water. We had to come off this hill down to the boardin' house. You know, honey [he says to Mother], where Arthur Barnes and them used to live, in that boardin' house. His mother run it, I think. [Mother nods.]
>
> You had to pump the water. It was an old pump and you had to pump the water and I was a-pumpin' away. That water tasted good man because it was good and cold. They'd let us come down there at recess, you see, and we'd get water to last from then to dinner [lunch].
>
> Anyway, I was a-pumpin' away and had my little old vinegar jug down there under the spout – I carried my water in a vinegar jug – and this boy come up and kicked it. His name was Dude, Dude Dyson. He was a bully-like feller. I told him not to do that no more and he kicked it again. I just took my jug by the ring and I slapped him around the side of the head with it and loped [jumped] him all at the same time. We went to wrestlin' around on the ground. We wrestled around long enough for some of them to run up the hill to the school and get the principal. He come down there and he separated us and got us up off the ground. He told us he wanted to see us after school. They [other students] told him what had happened. He didn't do nothin' to me but he kept Dude in after school.

Figure 2. Dad as a boy of about 10, the self-described "ol' country-looking boy."

I said that Dad grew up as the baby in the family, and that was true. But he was not the last born. The last child born to Grandpa and Grandma was a daughter, Helen Charlene. Little Charlene contracted both colitis and measles at about the same time. Her death was slow, painful, and heart wrenching for the family to watch. She was five years old.

Dad was always troubled by his sister's death, because he felt he had inadvertently contributed to it. "I took the measles first and had got over them and then gone back to school. And then she come down with the measles." I asked Dad if that was something that bothered him much. "Yeah, I thought about it a lot. But they wasn't nothin' I could do about it, honey. And then she took colitis on top of the measles and that's what killed her." Dad has a doleful and distant look in his eye as he says this.

The burden of this dark time was eased a bit by the tender mercies of a "colored family" that lived by the Ruths.

> Their last name was Olanger. Yeah, they lived right by us, right up behind us there at PV&K. Buddy, they was shore good people, real good people. I remember that they wouldn't let Mother and Dad do nothin'. Mother especially, they wouldn't let her do nothin'. Blanche was Mrs. Olanger's first name. They took care, cooked the food, cleaned the house, and done everything.

The ministrations of these fine people were sorely appreciated in that awful time.

Dad was a bit of a rowdy in those PV&K days, and not a little resourceful. Among his antics was a clever way he found to obtain some spending money. A distant relative ran a boarding house in Shields. The place had a wash house in a little building, with a stove on which water was heated for bathing. The men would hang their clothes while they bathed and Dad would take that opportunity to rifle their pockets for loose change.

From there, it was off to the Cook & Sharpe company store with his bounty. He would buy Cracker Jacks, as many boxes as his plunder could purchase. It wasn't so much that Dad liked Cracker Jacks. In fact, he wouldn't eat very much of the crunchy concoction at all. He was after something else:

I'd go under the warehouse where you'd take the stuff off the boxcars, where the train come in, the local train. And they'd put it in the warehouse there, you see, right across the railroad in front of the store.

I'd get up in under it there, in under the warehouse. I'd get me a bunch of Cracker Jacks, five or six boxes. I'd eat some of it but I'd get over there and just dump it out to get the prize out of it. I just wanted to see what the prize was.

Here is another of young Carl's stunts:

And I done something...let's see, the train had delivered the goods there and I'd help carry it then across the tracks and into the store. And I'd try to wait, get behind the rest of 'em you see, and we'd go through the store and they was a door like, a section of the counter that raised back. Well, you'd walk on through that and take the load in to the back of the store there.

Well, I'd come back out and if there wasn't nobody a-follerin' me close, I'd take off behind the counter and see if there was anything there I wanted to put in my pocket. Then I'd go get me another load of cases, you see. And if there was any scrip or anything a-layin' around the cash register that wasn't rung up, I'd latch onto it, buddy.

Mother, as she is listening to this is incredulous. "Carl, I can't believe you'd do that!" she remarks.

To this Dad replies, "Oh, they's a lot you don't know!"

We all just chuckle, and leave it at that.

At PV&K, Dad learned a valuable lesson from a skirmish that didn't turn out so well. Dad says:

Me and Chalk was down at the store, in front of PV&K store there. Well, this colored boy showed up that I didn't know and I guess I wanted to impress my big brother. I thought to myself, 'Well, I've got my big brother with me. I think I'll just work you over buddy, and make a showin' of it.' I figured if I got in trouble, Chalk would help me out. I figured wrong there!

I walked up to that boy and I said something, I don't remember what, and he told me, 'If you feel froggy, just hop!' Well, I hopped him and got him down. He went to snappin' at me, buddy, just like a snappin' dog! He was a-bitin' the fool out of me, man. I let that rascal up! I learned right there man, don't take on more than you can handle!

I asked Dad if he remembered the human terrier's name and in true Dad style he said, "Nooo! I didn't hang around to get his address, buddy!"

There was a funny aftermath to that skirmish that sounds just like Dad. You would think he'd had enough by this time, but something happened that caused that familiar anger of his to kick in.

Chalk walked up to me and was just a-laughin' out loud at me, buddy. I said, 'Why didn't you help me?!' Chalk said, 'Well Carl, they wasn't but one of 'em and he was your size. And besides, *you* jumped *him*! He wasn't a-doin' nothin' to you!' He was still a-laughin' at me and that made me mad, so I just loped [jumped on] him, buddy! Well, he was bigger than me and he let me have it! I got *bit up* by a stranger and *beat up* by my brother!

As we are talking, Mother ponders aloud where Dad got this tendency for anger and aggression. I actually ask Dad at this time, "Did Grandma ever sit you down and talk to you about how tightly you were wired?"

Dad replies, "No, she didn't tell me nothin' like that. She'd say 'Carl L., if I live til your daddy comes home from work, I'll tell him!' She'd threaten a lot."

Grandma would threaten more than she would follow through with, and with good reason. George Orville Ruth was stern (to put it mildly) in meting out discipline, as the following story shows:

> We was livin' up on the hill and a bunch of us boys and girls were down in the alley at the bottom of the hill playin' baseball. They called me 'Little Babe Ruth' [a distant relative, by the way], and that made me feel big.
>
> I heard Dad whistle and that meant he was callin' one of us when we was out. When we heard that, buddy, we'd sprint home, no matter where we was or what we was a-doin'.
>
> I got up to the house and Dad says, 'Carl L., your mother and your sis [Emma] are going up to Benito [between Evarts and Highsplint] now, so you stay here and play around the house where I'll know where you are.'
>
> I said, 'Okay Poppa.'

But his dad had hardly turned his back when young Carl bolted back down the hill to his friends and the ballgame! Dad says, "Well, I hadn't much more than got back down the hill until I hear that whistle again. I thanks, 'Well, I've had it now!'"

Dad gets home and is met with a short but stern lecture, which ended with the command that he stay around the house to do his playing. Believe it or not, the recalcitrant Carl's next words are as follows.

"Well I caught him busy again and straight back down that hill I took!"

My incredulous response was, "Same day?!"

"Yeaaah, same day! Same game!"

This was another of those times when Mother, Dad, and I sat around the table laughing until we had tears in our eyes. Dad picks up the story:

Well, he whistled again and man, I knowed that I'd had it! I went runnin' back home again. He said, 'What did I tell you, Carl L.?!' I said, 'You told me not to go back down there no more, Poppa.'

He said, 'Well, what did you do it for?!'

I said [timidly], 'Just cause.'

He said, 'Dammit, cause why?!' And I seen he had in his hand behind him his bank belt, his mine bank belt. [A bank belt is a wide leather belt intended to provide a modicum of back support for the working miner.]

I seen that thing and I thanks, 'Lord have mercy. If he hits me with that thing he'll kill me!'

Well, they was a bed settin' right there in the front room, an old iron bed. The rockin' chair was like, over here, and I was standin' close to it.

He said, 'I told you not to go back down there!' He rared back with that bank belt and hit me. I thanks, 'Well, if he hits me again I've had it!' I dove to the floor before it ever got to me that second time and he caught the arm of that rockin' chair. He jerked arm, brace, and all off that chair with that bank belt, buddy! I mean, plumb off!

Well, I dove for the floor and I took off up in under that bed, buddy. I had a slingshot in my right hip pocket and the cockeyed fork of that slingshot caught on the foot of that bed and left my rear hangin' out. He hit me across the tail and I ripped pocket and all off a-gettin' up in under that bed!

He said, 'Come out of there!' Well, I had to. I come out a snifflin.' When I come out he set in on me again, buddy.

I never will forget what I did after that. I went outside and got a hatchet. I took that slingshot that got hung on the bed and chopped that thing into a hundred pieces, buddy. I took it out on that slingshot!

PV&K was nearly the end of the Carl L. E. Ruth story. This wasn't because of the above run-in with his father, but on account of illness. In a short span of time Dad had the measles, pneumonia, and typhoid fever.

All my hair come out when I had typhoid fever.[10] I was so sick, man. They give me up to die at that point. They said Doc Lewis told 'em if I wasn't no better the next mornin' I wasn't going to make it. Doc Lewis told 'em he'd done all he could do. He had give me up to die.

Dad did get a little better by the next morning, but it was touch and go for a while. He goes on to recount a story from this critical point in his young life:

Mother had to go to the pump at the foot of the hill to get water. She said to me, 'Now honey, you lay in bed.' I was still bedridden with typhoid fever. Well, I could smell Mother's cookin' in the kitchen. She had a ham in a big pot on top of the stove. I could smell that ham a-cookin' on that ham bone. I waited, to give her time to get out, and I kindly [kind of] drug myself into the kitchen. I was walkin' but kindly draggin' myself for I was so weak, you see.

Well, I got the lid off that pot and I was a-tryin' to fork the meat out of that pot. Well, I got it out and got it on top of the stove cabinet. You know what a stove cabinet is? It's covered in porcelain. I got the meat on that, and I was so weak I dropped to the floor. I pulled myself up and I gouged me a bite or two off of that ham. I looked and I seen poor ol' Mother coming back up the hill with the water. I didn't have time to clean the mess up or nothing but I was able to flop that ham back in the kettle and put the lid on it. I crawled back to the bed. Doc Lewis told them to not let me eat solid food, you see, but I was so hungry.

Dad sums up his early years by saying, "Buddy, I've been a cracker jack!" In light of the earlier story from the PV&K store I shared with you, I thought that a choice phrase.

––––––––––––––––––

The Ruths next move to Draper (community just west of Evarts) because Grandpa gets a better job at the Draper mine. Dad is in the fifth grade at this time and only he, Ed, and Chalk live at home now. The older siblings – Lawrence, Emma, and Ervin – are all married by this time.

Dad and his family have now traveled from Washburn, Tennessee, in and around Middlesboro, Shields, and now Draper, Kentucky. While there were more relocations to come, none after the move to Shields was significant in terms of cultural change for the family. From Shields on, all the moves are in Harlan County.

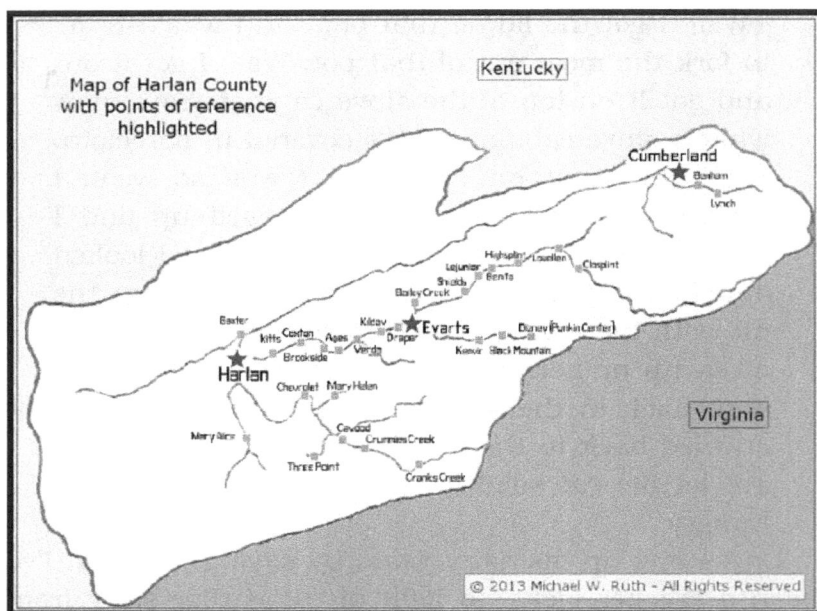

Figure 3. Harlan County sites of relevance

Dad grew from child to adolescent while living in Draper. These were the years of the Great Depression (though Dad's running joke was "I never could figure out what was so *great* about it!"). The Depression years were hard for Dad. He would often say, "The Democrats blamed Hoover and the Republicans blamed Roosevelt. I don't know who it was, but somebody liked to starved me to death!"

Necessity brought creativity, and Dad found a way to get a little money in his pocket while a Depression-era boy in Draper. A neighbor woman would frequently give Dad money to go to the store and buy her fifty cents worth of new potatoes. Dad would pocket the fifty cents and go to a nearby potato patch a man owned and stealthily dig up roughly fifty cents worth of new potatoes. He would clean them good, put them in a "poke" and take them to the neighbor, fifty cents the richer!

Dad caught and ate a lot of fish during the Depression. He didn't need a fishing rod, he would just cut him a sapling for that, and make him a "fishin' pole." But tackle was costly and he either didn't have or didn't want to waste money on that. Ingenious, even when young, he would make a hook out of a safety pin and would plait sewing thread for line. Dad says:

> Buddy, that was hard fishin'. Of course a safety pin don't have a barb on it like a hook and wasn't strong metal, and that sewin' thread was easy to break. You had to really work a fish to get it in!

> Nobe Farley was the night watchman at the mines. Me and him had us a deal. I'd catch him a mess of fish when I was a-catchin' mine, and he'd give me enough grease [lard] to fry mine in. We'd trade fish for grease, you see. I was about twelve or fourteen at the time.

To his dying day Dad absolutely hated to wait in line for anything, and he simply would not do it at all if avoidable. Here's why:

> In the Depression we'd get commodities. Word would get out that they was a load of commodities comin' in. They'd ship 'em to the depot in Harlan, you see. They'd come in maybe every two or three weeks, I think. I don't remember now. Everybody down through there from Harlan to Evarts would take off to Harlan, buddy. We'd walk down there,

walk from Draper to Harlan. It's about eight miles. You'd finally get there and Lord have mercy they'd be a big line. I've lined up from up past the New Harlan Theater [South Main Street] just to get in line. That line would go from there, down across the bridge, to that big building there on the right [Hackney Distributors] close to the railroad crossin'. That buildin' is where they'd give out the commodities. I'd say that line would be about a quarter of a mile!

When you finally got in the building you'd get the allotment of whatever stuff they had. You didn't pass on nothin', buddy! I carried mine home in a grass [burlap] sack I'd bring with me. Once I got what I could, I'd take off a-walkin' then, them eight miles back home. We walked the tracks most of the time, you see, for that was the shortest distance. It'd cut out all them hills and curves.

They's been many a time I've got right up there near the door, buddy, and they'd be give out of stuff. See, they'd just have so much of this or that – fruit, rice, cheese, powdered milk, dried beans, sugar, flour, meal, stuff like that – and when they give out of each of what they had, well, that was that! They'd be run out. They'd say come back on such-and-such a day and we'll have more in. They'd just give out. You've walked all that way and pulled that long line for nothin'! That's why I say, buddy, I ain't standin' in no more lines! I've pulled that shift! [In the last quarter of his life, Dad hated to go to a restaurant for lunch after church. There is usually a line to stand in.]

You could tell when they'd give out grapefruit. [He starts laughing as he tells this, recalling memories.] You'd see a few hulls scattered here and there as you walked back home. The further you got, the deeper them grapefruit hulls got along there. People'd get tempered to 'em, you see. We didn't eat a lot of grapefruit up in there and it took 'em one or two to get tempered to 'em. Once they did, they'd just eat the whole bag! You could tell when they'd eat up all the grapefruit because the hulls would go to thinning out along the track or road again til they was plumb gone, buddy!

I asked what he would do if he got near the building and they had run out of everything? Dad laughingly says, "You'd just turn and walk sadly away."

Following is another of those stories which shows the better angels of Dad's nature. He was about thirteen at the time of its unfolding.

Later on they got to deliverin' the commodities to the Evarts depot, so those of us that lived down that way didn't have to make that long haul afoot into Harlan. When they come in, I'd walk to the depot from Draper [about a mile] and get mine. I'd bring it home in a grass sack just like I did when I'd go to Harlan.

Our neighbor was Paris Parr. He was in his mid-thirties and he was crippled and couldn't walk. He couldn't get out to get his commodities. Well, when I got back with mine, I'd then go get his identification card [required, or one could simply loop through the line two or three times] and then head back to the Evarts depot to pick his up for him.

Though they lived in Draper, Dad went to school at Evarts, as all Draper children did in middle and high school. He was placed in the sixth grade because it was determined he was too advanced for the fifth. Although Dad had no great amount of formal education (he left school after the eighth grade to work), he was a smart boy and man. In terms of just natural, innate intelligence, Dad was quite likely the smartest person I have ever known.

Leaving school early was not that uncommon for rural boys at that time. Any young man fortunate enough to find a job took it. Dad found a job. He went to work in the Draper mine when he was 15 years old. Because he was so young, Grandpa had to sign his permission for him to go to work. For the next twenty-eight years of his life, Dad would be a miner.

At the Draper mine Grandpa was initially a blacksmith. Later on, he was a brattice man [brattice cloth is used to direct the air flow in the mine] and a timber man. This was about the time that the UMWA [United Mine Workers of America, the miners' union] came to the area and, as Dad puts it, "Dad secretly joined the union. You kept it under your hat, then." Dangerous times.

Although Grandpa was a miner, as was his custom, he picked up extra money doing carpentry work. His most memorable woodworking job at Draper was a charitable project, however. Dad helped Grandpa on this job.

A relative of Roy Colston died and the family wanted Grandpa to build their loved one a black walnut casket. It was beautiful, as Dad recalls. Given the natural quality and character of that particular hardwood, I imagine it certainly was. This job was done as a gift to the Colstons for neither Grandpa nor Dad would have dreamed of accepting payment for such work.

(This was actually the second casket Dad constructed with Grandpa. In Columbia, they built a diminutive coffin for an unfortunate family who had lost an infant. They lined this one with satin, in consideration of its tender inhabitant.)

––––––––––––––––––––

We are driving through Kildav (just west of Draper) on one of our research trips when Dad casually says "Now, right here honey is where I was a-hitchhikin' with that corpse." (If the reader would like to approximate my experience when Dad said this, you should hear the needle of a phonograph scratching loudly across the face of a record about now!)

"Wait...this is where you did WHAT?!"

"Where I hitchhiked with a corpse," Dad says nonchalantly.

I pulled over and clicked the recorder. I wasn't about to miss anything on this one!

> This feller in Draper had died you see. I remember, it was a real poor family. You've heard of puttin' somebody in a pine box? Well, they had him in a rough ol' pine box. Me and – who was it … I can't remember now – was gonna bury the feller for them people. We felt so sorry for 'em for they was grievin' so, and they was dirt poor.

Well, we took off out of Draper a-carryin' that casket down through there. I believe the street we went up was Wade Street, but I'm not sure. By the time we got up to the main road that ol' casket was about to come apart. I guess it was just from the shakin' of us carryin' it by hand all the way up through there. You could see the corpse in it through some of the cracks, they was so big.

When we got up to the main road we decided to hitchhike to Kildav 'cause we was afraid that casket was gonna come completely apart on us. Well, we caught a ride with a lumber truck. He had been deliverin' timbers to one of the mines. He had some rope on the back of his truck and he give us some to tie up that casket so it didn't come apart. We tied the casket up the best we could, and then put it up in the back of that truck. He let us out there where Doc Lewis lived. That's where we buried him. We carried him up to that old graveyard there up on the hill between Draper and Kildav and buried him in that little cemetery up there.

––––––––––––––––––

The family moved from Draper, a move which took them to the shotgun house (no longer there) at the bell crossing (where the railroad tracks cross the road) in Evarts. The Ruths lived there just a few months. This was a beneficial move for the family because Grandpa had secured jobs for himself, Lawrence, Ed, Chalk, and Dad at the Black Mountain Mine.[11]

Uncle Ed had married and was living in Draper where, eventually, he built his own house. He moved a number of times within Draper before building his house, and Dad had a yarn about that. He said that Uncle Ed "had moved so many times that when his chickens saw him coming they would just lay down and cross their legs, a-waitin' for Ed to tie them up for the move!"

Not long after that, Chalk married Rosa Bailey, and moved out. In a few months, Dad, who was the only child at home now, secured better housing in Bailey Creek (just beyond Evarts, and which I only ever heard called "Baileys" Creek) for himself and his parents, and they moved there.

Interestingly, the newlyweds, Chalk and Rosa, rented rooms in the home of the Vaughn family, which you will read about shortly. Mr. Vaughn was deceased at this time and the family consisted of Laura Vaughn and her three daughters, Goldie, Della, and Dollie. Chalk loved to hear the Vaughn girls sing and Della remembers he would call to them from his living room, "Hey girls, sing me a song!" Their selection was usually one of the old familiar hymns. Chalk and his wife loved those early married days, living in the Vaughn home.

As for Dad, the most significant change ever to come to his life would initiate while he lived at Bailey Creek. It would have nothing to do with mining. He would begin dating a girl he had known for some time. Several months later they would marry.

Coal-yard Facts

The first documented use of coal in the state of Kentucky was in 1750 by Dr. Thomas Walker.

CHAPTER 4

Carl and Della

In 1937, Dad lived at Bailey Creek with his Mom and Dad. He was their financial caretaker at the time, as Grandpa was now disabled. Dad was mining at Black Mountain's 31 Mine. In fact, except for bookends of time that can be measured in scant months, the entirety of Dad's twenty-eight year mining career will be spent at the 31 Mine.

In that same year Dad falls in love with a seventeen-year-old girl from one of the finest families you would ever hope to know. Laura Vaughn lived on Evarts Hill with her three daughters. Goldie was the eldest, then came Della, and then Dollie, her youngest. A tighter and more lovingly-bonded family you will never see.

The Vaughns had known their own tragedy and sorrow. A fourth daughter, Edna, was born to Henry and Laura in April of 1919. She was the second child in birth order, and was not long for this world. Edna was stricken with meningitis and died the year after her birth, in October of 1920. She was 18 months old. Edna is interred in the Burkhart Cemetery, high off Laurel Lane, in Evarts.

As tragic as the loss of little Edna was, the Vaughns would know a still darker day. But that is a story for a later chapter.

Dad and his parents moved from Bailey Creek to Coxton (about 3.5 miles east of Harlan). Although this takes him farther away from work, Dad liked Coxton better and wanted to live there. The Coxton community was home to two mining camps. To the left across the Coxton bridge (which spans the Clover Fork Branch of the Cumberland River) was the camp for the Chevrolet Mine[12] (located roughly halfway between Harlan and Cawood, in a hollow off to the left, traveling toward Cawood). To the center and right was one of the camps for the Black Mountain Mines. As a Black Mountain miner, Dad had rented one of those houses for himself and his parents.

Dad begins dating Goldie Vaughn in early 1937. Their activities are typical of dating couples. They go to the diner, roller skating, and to the movies in Black Mountain (yes, Black Mountain had its own theater then), Evarts, or Harlan. The pastime Dad definitely enjoys most, though, is spending time at the Vaughn home. The warm and welcoming environment there is not lost on him, nor is the fact that Laura is an excellent cook! In addition, his brother Chalk (and wife Rosa) are renting rooms from the Vaughns, as previously noted. This allows the brothers to spend time together in the evenings.

One night, Dad has a date set with Goldie. As usual with Dad, there is a story within that story. Goldie had something else she wanted to do that night and really wasn't into a date night.

"Why don't you go in my place, Della?" she says to her younger sister.

"What?!" Della replies. "He's your boyfriend, not mine!"

"It's you he likes, Della. He's only dating me to be around you!"

This is news to Della. As it turns out, however, Goldie is right. (Had she been more astute – or interested – Della might have discerned this from the fact that when Carl comes in with a box of candy, it is she, not Goldie he hands the candy to!) Della fills in for her older sister that night and from then on, it is she Carl dates.

Several months after that initial date, Carl and Della marry (August 13, 1938). They were married in Harlan, in the office of the Fuller Furniture Store on the corner of 1st and Central. This odd arrangement transpired because Carl had accidentally left the intended minister's name and address in the wrong pair of pants. When they get to town, he can remember neither the reverend's name nor where he lives! A friend he bumps into in Harlan tells him of a Baptist minister he had just seen in the barbershop. That friend goes for the preacher (Rev. W. Clayton Longworth), who is just leaving the shop, and asks him if he will perform the ceremony. He consents to do so. In the meantime, Carl somehow secures the Fuller Furniture Store as an alternate location. Roy Alfred, the butcher at the company store in Coxton and Ruby Stringer, also of Coxton, were friends of theirs who served as witnesses.

———————————

Once married, Dad, and now Mother, continue to live briefly in the house he rented in Coxton. It had to be hard for a young bride to move into that house with a matriarch already in place. As was her way though, Mother would make the best of it.

Just days after they are married, Mother will find out what she is in for as a miner's wife. Dad comes in early from work one day. He isn't wearing his bank (mining) clothes, which is to say he has showered at the mine bathhouse and changed before coming home, as was the custom. She notices his left thumb is bandaged.

I said, 'Oh God, Carl! What's happened?' He sat me down and told me the story. He had been cutting timbers for placement in the mine. They used an ax for that. He was down on his knees and was using the rail to rest the timbers on as he cut them. The handle of the ax caught the other rail and that threw his stroke off just enough to cause him to hit his thumb instead of the timber. He was holding the timber in place with his left hand to cut it with his right hand, see. When the ax handle hit the rail, it changed his stroke. He cut most of his thumb off, from just below the knuckle joint on up.

Carl just insisted that he show me that thumb. I said, 'Shoooo no, Carl. I don't want to see it!' But he just would have it that I see that thumb. He unbandaged it and showed it to me. It was all stitched up and awful looking. I mean, the doctor had done a good job, but it was just awful looking.

Dad was bathed and in his clean clothes because after cutting more than half his thumb off, he actually took the time to go to the bathhouse and shower (which was his normal routine at shift's end). He then went to the Black Mountain Hospital, where Dr. Geninie treated and stitched his injury.

This accident occurred just shortly after Mother and Dad were married. Mother didn't know it at the time, but this would be the first in a series of harrowing experiences that will, from time to time, mark their first thirty years together.

Mother tells a funny story from those early days. Grandma Ruth had gone to Shields to spend a couple of nights with her daughter Emma. Mother realized this meant the cooking duty would be hers for the next couple of days. She says, "I couldn't sleep that night – no kidding – for worrying about having to make scratch biscuits for breakfast the next morning." Problem is, she didn't know how! Presenting her creation at the table, she watched as Dad and Grandpa began to eat. My Grandfather loved Mother and doted on her. (He once said to Grandma, "This one's mine. The rest of the daughter-in-laws are yours.") He also loved to tease her but, sensing how important this was to Mother, boy did he brag on those biscuits! So did Dad.

In a short while, Mother asks, "Carl, were my biscuits really good?" Dad is caught in that awkward space that challenges the old maxim about honesty being the best policy.

As gently as he could, Dad replies, "No, honey. They was pretty rough."

Mother, ever the sensitive soul, cried a good cry over that! "I was so embarrassed by them biscuits after he told me that," she says.

This story is remarkable to me because, by the time I came along, Mother was a fine cook and breakfast was her specialty. In fact, when our own two children were young, their greatest anticipation when we would come for a visit was waking to one of "Mamaw's breakfasts." (They were also partial to the Little Debbie cakes she kept in the sweets drawer!)

Shortly after they were married Mother and Dad move to their own place in Coxton. They move into a duplex and live above a Mrs. Hampton and her daughter Betsy. The company-owned duplexes each had four rooms – two up, two down. "Mrs. Hampton said she didn't need her upstairs rooms, so she rented them to Carl and me." Like all of the Black Mountain company houses, the house was painted white and trimmed in green. Their first child, my oldest sister Patricia, was born in that house. (At the time of this writing that duplex is still occupied.)

Mother recalls a particular gathering that took place in late October in 1941, in Coxton. My sister Pat was just a toddler at the time:

There was a Halloween get-together down at the Coxton Theater building. The theater was no longer there. Me and Mom [my maternal grandmother] and Pat had walked down there. Carl had gone on ahead. When we got inside there was a crowd gathered around somebody in the middle of the floor. I knew right then it was Carl!

He had dressed up like Li'l Abner and he was entertaining the crowd. He was sitting on his butt right in the middle of the floor. He was acting like he was having a hard time getting his shoes on and laced up. Everybody was laughing up a storm!

The typical workday in Coxton began at 4:30 a.m., when a miner's home came to life. Dad would stoke the cook stove fire so Mother could get to making breakfast while he was readying for work. Once Dad was off she would clean the kitchen, do other housework, maybe run to the company store. Her sister Dollie, who was married to J. T. Latham at the time, lived in Coxton too, and Mother would visit with her or other friends. "We'd sit on the porch and talk and chat with friends as they passed by, walking down the road." Mother typically began preparing "supper" about 3:30 or so, and Dad would get home from work sometime before 5:00. After she finished the dishes, they would sit on the porch and talk with neighbors. Mother adds, "We would read in the evening too. I liked to read comic books and Carl liked to read Westerns."

Not long after Pat was born, the family moved to another duplex on the same road but closer to the Coxton bridge. More room was needed and they now had one full apartment in the duplex. The two rooms downstairs were kitchen and living room. Upstairs consisted of two bedrooms.

Occupying the other apartment in the new duplex were Charlie and Jessie McMillen, and their children. Mrs. McMillen, or "Mac," became one of Mother's dearest Coxton friends (along with Carma Lou Marino).

I have a vague memory of Mrs. McMillen myself, as she occasionally came to visit Mother when we lived in Harlan. I recall two salient points about her. First, I remember her as a very gracious and dignified lady, a "proper" lady, to borrow a good old phrase. Mother often said, "Mac could put on a print dress and she would look all dressed up. She just carried herself so well." The other thing I remember about Mrs. McMillen is her hands. By the early 1960s, she had debilitating arthritis, with the accompanying inflamed knuckles and fingers drawn askew. I remember thinking as a child that her malady must hurt terribly.

Mrs. McMillen was as remarkable a woman as she was dignified. After the Coxton years the McMillen family moved to Cumberland, Kentucky. Mrs. McMillen, by then in her thirties with four children, decided she wanted to earn a degree and become a school teacher. She graduated from Cumberland College and, true to her dream, became a teacher.

While a student, the ravages of crippling arthritis had already set in. Mrs. McMillen typed her research papers and other assignments on a manual typewriter by depressing the keys with a pencil. Her fingers were no longer dexterous and nimble enough to work the keys.

As mentioned, Mrs. McMillen visited Mother from time-to-time when we lived in Harlan. One day, on just such a visit, the two women ride into town and Mother recounts the following:

> Mac had to take some business papers into the courthouse for something. I don't recall what it was about. She was still able to drive in those days. When we got out she was trying to put some change in the parking meter. She was struggling so. I said, 'Mac, let me do that.' She said, 'No Della, I want to do it. I want to use my hands as long as I can.' It took her some, but she got that change in there. It hurt me to watch that,

because she meant so much to me. I hated to see her suffer like that.

She was really something, I'm telling you. She never complained and she just had the best, strongest spirit about her.

Although the mines of the Black Mountain Coal Company were union mines, occasionally there would be a work stoppage while a new contract was negotiated, or for some other dispute between company and union. During those times, Dad would scout the bottomlands and mountains for shagbark, pignut, and shellbark hickories. Hickory wood is strong, hard yet flexible, and as a result of the latter characteristic, shock resistant. All this combines to make it the excellent choice for tool handles. Dad would take hickory and carve it into handmade handles for ax, pick, shovel, hammer, and other implements. He would sell them to anyone who wanted them, but mainly to the miners of Chevrolet and Black Mountain who lived in Coxton, and the other men of that community. Dad sold his hammer handles for a quarter. Ax, pick, and shovel handles pulled fifty cents.

Good experiences came Dad's way often in Coxton, and good experiences meant good stories, like the following.

Frank and Joe Benge were brothers Dad had known since the late 1920s. They mined together at 31. He had a couple of good stories about his two friends, which were among his favorites:

> They was kindly out of the backwoods, Frank and Joe. One day, they figured they'd go to the show at the Evarts theater [the Roslyn Theater]. This was in the early '30s. The theater was

showin' a western. Well, the outlaws was on the run and the law was a-chasin' on horses. The outlaws went up in a rock outcroppin'. The posse had surrounded them and they was headed for a shootout. They was a big rock there one of the outlaws was sneakin' around. He was gonna back shoot one of the law.

Frank jumped up from his seat and hollered, 'There he is! He's a-comin' around that rock!' Well, Frank just thought he couldn't get that lawman's attention because he [the lawman] wasn't payin' him no mind.

So, Frank just pulled out his pistol, buddy, and shot the outlaw! He shot plumb through the theater screen, buddy!

It strikes me that this would be just about the right time to invoke Mark Twain's observation about truth being stranger than fiction. In the case of Harlan County in those days, it was often a *lot* stranger. And it was a heck of a lot funnier!

Here is another example:

Me and Chalk was diggin' coal and Chalk said 'I'm goin' to get Joe Benge to come over here and dig with us.' [These were the pick and shovel days.] Chalk, a-raggin' at me, said 'I'll put you in the middle and Joe can work one end and I'll work the other.'

I says, 'Huh-uh, nooooo. That dog won't hunt!' I said, 'You can get in the middle and Joe on the far side, and I'll work over here by myself!'

Joe was a good guy but he talked all the time. He'd talk to his self even. He did that all the time. If you wasn't a-payin' attention to him he'd say,

'Well dammit, you don't have to talk to me. I'll just talk to myself!' And he would, buddy!

We was sittin' there a-waitin' for a trip to come in – you know, coal cars – so we could start loadin' coal. Well, Joe was runnin' low of carbide for his lamp. He reached back in the hip pocket of his overalls to get his carbide flask.

Well, Joe went to cussin' and raisin' Cain and Chalk said, 'Joe, if you don't settle down, I'm gonna knock you in the head. I'm gonna tie you up and load you in one of these bank cars and ship you out!' He was just a-goin' on with Joe, you know. Chalk says, 'What on earth's wrong with you, Joe?'

Joe said, 'I've told that damn woman a half-dozen times to patch my hip pocket and she ain't patched it yet. Now I've lost ever last bit of my qyarbide [carbide]! That's how he pronounced it, 'qyar-bide.'

Me and Chalk was just a-laughin' at his carryin' on and one of us said, 'Well buddy, I guess you'll just have to mine in the dark!' We was just a-kiddin' of course. We give him some carbide in a minute.

Dad's brother Chalk loved to get Joe riled up about this or that as they worked. He got such a kick out of Joe's antics once he got up to speed, which didn't take long. Dad, Chalk, and Joe were sitting at the face of the coal (coal yet to be mined), waiting for a trip of cars and Chalk took this as an opportunity to get Joe lathered up.

It seems Frank, Joe's brother, tended to sprinkle his conversation liberally with curse words, which Chalk knew agitated Joe (even though Joe did likewise, as these stories illustrate). He utilized that to get Joe up and running, and soon Joe was complaining about his brother's cursing, and how it troubled him so. Dad picks the story up here:

> Chalk says, 'Joe, why don't you pray for your brother Frank, buddy?' I knowed what Chalk was a-doin', you see. He was gettin' ol' Joe a-goin'. [Dad begins to chuckle telling this. It is clear he is reliving it as he talks.] Joe says, 'Chalk, prayin' ain't doin' no good, buddy. I've prayed enough to save ten sonsabitches like him. Prayin' won't help him!' Me and Chalk are just crackin' up! Joe said, 'I've just took to prayin' "Lord, have mercy on him, and if you can't have mercy on him, just kill the ignorant thang!"'

Dad and Chalk were rolling with laughter. Chalk got exactly what he was hoping for!

Though Joe likely said it the way he did for its comic effect as much as anything, there is little doubt he was being somewhat earnest. Dad remembers encountering a similar applied theology in church once as a young man. The sermon ended, the minister was giving an altar call, to which no one was responding. In frustration the pastor said to the congregation, "What's the matter with you. Don't any of you want to go to Heaven?" No one moved. He makes a further plea. Still no response. The frustrated minister cries out, "Well you can all just go to hell then!" With that, he stormed out of the church!

After Frank Benge quit mining he became a carpenter. Dad had this big black tool chest that I can remember as long as I've been alive. Frank Benge made that chest for Dad. My brother Ronnie now has it.

Mother and Dad had an active social life in Coxton. They had many friends, most of whom were fellow miners and their wives. They went dancing on the weekend at the clubhouse in Coxton[13] – a fine place it was in the day. The local Baptist church was in eyeshot of their home and Mother and Dad walked to church there on Sundays.

Mother passes on a brief story about Dad from those days in Coxton and the Baptist church. At Christmas Dad would play Santa Claus for the children of Coxton. Mother says "When the evening was over Carl would be just rolling with sweat. All that padding and that hot suit just burned him up. He loved playing Santa for the kids but he sure was glad to get home and get out of that outfit!"

A key aspect of the social life in Coxton was the amateur baseball team.[14] While these weren't professional teams, the game was taken seriously by the players and fans and some hardcore baseball was played. (The big mining operation in Lynch had a stadium that would have rivaled a lot of minor league ball parks.) Many of the mining communities had their own team. Dad, of course, played for Coxton. There was a Closplint team, a Shields, a Kenvir, a Highsplint, and so on. Teams characteristically and proudly had the name of their community/coal camp prominently displayed on the chest of their uniform.

Dad was a lifelong lover of baseball. He taught me the game when I was very young. I can remember as a young boy sitting together on Saturday watching the "Game of the Week," on ABC. He and I were Yankee fans and those amazing teams they fielded in the sixties (with the likes of Berra, Pepitone, Richardson, Mantle, and Maris) are still a part of my fond childhood memories.

In his later years, Dad rooted for the Cincinnati Reds. He had a very Dad-like reason for doing so. He appreciated the fact that they had a "clean-cut" look, allowing neither flowing locks nor facial hair. That was Dad.

I loved hearing him tell the stories of the baseball games the camp teams would have back in the day. Dad was an equal opportunity humorist. He would tell stories on himself as readily as on anyone else. This is one of his baseball memories:

> I played right field. And buddy, I could fly. Anything hit from right center on, I got to it – and I'd catch it! If I got to it, I caught it, buddy. In fact, and this is the God's truth, if a fly was hit anywhere between right center and anywhere in right field, my teammates just started trottin' off the field. They knowed I had it, buddy!
>
> But I couldn't hit for spit! Ain't that somethin' for somebody kin to the Babe! I couldn't hit nothin'. If I did luck up and hit it I'd get on base, for I could fly. But Lord have mercy, I couldn't hit nothin'!

Dad had experiences that were either so bizarre or so funny (and often bizarrely funny) that I sometimes am pressed to believe they came his way just so he could share them. Here is one such story involving his Coxton baseball buddies, but not a baseball game:

> I was comin' home from the mines one day after work, in my T Model Ford. I had an old T Model at the time. I got to the crossin' there at the Brookside mine[15] and buddy, out of nowhere come this ol' boar hog a-shootin' across the road. It had broke out of its pen somewhere.

I was fixin' to swerve my car, but they was a truck unloadin' at the company store there at Brookside. He had backed in you see, and his nose was kindly stickin' out on the road a little. I thanks, 'Well, better to hit that hog than that truck!' I swerved and hit that hog and knocked him down and he rolled right up in under my car.

A T Model sits high up off the road, you see. Well, that hog got back up on its legs somehow and when he did, he raised the front end of that T Model plumb off the road! That hog was kindly addled I guess, and it took off, buddy. It was a-headin' right for the railroad tracks with me and that T Model on its back! Well, he finally run out from under me and I dropped down and come to a stop. He took off a-runnin' up through there just a-squealin'!

Some of my Coxton baseball buddies, Alb Anderson, Roy Alfred, Les Owens, and some more of 'em was sittin' there on the porch of the store just a-rollin' they was laughin' so hard! One of 'em hollered out, 'Carl, you ain't hurt him none. There he goes!' I said, 'Hell, I ain't carin' nothin' about him. I was just wonderin' where he was a-takin' me!

Mother and Dad have fond memories of the Coxton years. We talked about this period of their lives many times in preparation for this book. These were endearing years, years filled with good times and good friends. They were not, however, halcyon days. This era had its share of hardship too, as we shall see next.

Figure 4. Mother, Dad, and my sister Pat in Coxton in 1941. Neighbor's car and house in background.

CHAPTER 5

Struggle and Sacrifice

The first half of the twentieth century was a dark time for Appalachian miners. Actually, the story begins even decades earlier, in the mid-1800s. Kentucky's own money men and barons from the Northeast and Midwest (and even some from England) had descended and stripped the hills of virgin timber. They scratched railroads deep into the mountains to remove that timber and thereby changed the inherent culture of Southern Appalachia forever. Before long, many of these same industrialists and their successors discovered that the wealth *on* the mountains (native timber) was nothing when compared to the wealth that lay *within* the mountains. Industry ran on machinery and that machinery ran on coal.

Local businessman Jesse Blanton railed the first train of coal[16] out of Harlan County (mined in Terry's Fork, shipped out from Wallins Creek) in August of 1911. Since that first load of coal railed out of Harlan County on that L&N train, some six billion tons of the "black diamond" have been extracted from Eastern Kentucky (more than a billion tons from Harlan County alone). That's a lot of coal, which translates to, that's a lot of money. The same avarice exhibited by the timber barons was clearly evident in the coal magnates, and to a maniacal scale. The profits were massive,[17] and they intended to share as little of it as possible.

The mining strife was about power, ultimately. The companies had it – all of it – and did not want to share it. In the early years, what they did give up wasn't given at all. It had to be taken. The war to unionize the mines is well known to all who are remotely informed. Harlan County was a, if not *the*, hotspot in that war.

As earlier noted, my Grandpa Ruth, once he became a miner, quietly joined the UMWA. In those early years it had to be done secretly, as the union had no foothold at all. As I have said, no foothold meant no power. A miner who joined the union in the 1920s was taking the well-being of his family, if not his very life, in his hands.

As you now know, Dad became a miner when he was fifteen years old. He joined the UMWA not long afterwards. "I signed up at a [union] meeting in Columbus Ball's garage. It was there on Snuff Street,[18] in Evarts. That's where we had our meetings. That's where I took my obligations." (Interestingly, this same building, Mr. Ball's garage, had earlier played a crucial role in my Mother's life, as we shall later see.)

These were dark and dangerous days in the world of Appalachian coal. Writers wrote about it, singers sang about it (most famously, *Sixteen Tons*), and miners and coal operators fought.

Before moving the story forward, this is a fitting place to include a needed word of explanation. Later in this chapter you are going to read about the collusion existing between Harlan County government in the early to mid-twentieth century and the coal operators. I want to say a word here about that latter group, the coal operators. From just prior to WWI on, the Harlan County mining industry changed significantly as smaller mines were either bought, marginalized, or forced out of business by powerful conglomerates with deep pockets. To be sure, there were still mines operating which were locally owned and operated. But the heavy hitters in Harlan coal were now the industrial and financial giants in the North.

In fact, we are talking about some of the biggest names ever to exist in American industry and wealth. The names just might surprise you. Among their ranks were J. P. Morgan, Cyrus McCormick, Jr., Andrew Mellon, Francis Peabody, and Henry Ford. Some of the parent companies ultimately behind the coal operations in Harlan County were U. S. Steel – via their subsidiary U. S. Coal and Coke (Lynch), Fordson Coal Company and Henry Ford (Wallins Creek), Peabody Coal Company (Black Mountain), North American [Detroit] Edison (King Harlan Mines), Mellon Corporation (Elkhorn-Piney Coal Company), International Harvester (Benham), and the Commonwealth Power Corporation of New York (Kentucky King).[19] Ultimately, this was the kind of men and muscle behind the coal operators of Harlan County. This gives the reader some idea of what the miners were up against.

The most famous of the coal conflicts in Harlan County occurred on May 5, 1931, and is known as the Battle of Evarts.[20] Mining wages, already lower than that of the union miners in the northern coal states, dropped 39% from 1929-1931. The tipping point came in February of 1931, when the operators imposed yet another pay cut. This time, a 10% reduction was enacted.[21]   By the time of the Battle of Evarts, the average Harlan County miner was making just under $750.00 annually. Be sure you read that correctly. That's seven-hundred-and-fifty-dollars a year! It works out to $14.42 per week, given a 52-week work year (they did not get vacation leave). And miners in other Kentucky counties were commonly making even less. In fact, once company deductions were taken from earnings, it was not uncommon for a miner to draw no pay whatsoever. And it even gets worse.

Not satisfied with just having miners work for slave wages, in those early days most nonunion coal companies found even more ways to cheat them. Here are but a few of the means they employed to accomplish this:

- Miners were forced to pay for the dynamite used in blasting the company's coal from the face of the seam.
- They had to pay for the coal oil for their headlamps and for the oil for the lamps to see and work by. In later years, they had to pay for the carbide for those lights and still later, they had to pay rent on the battery-powered headlamps.
- They loaded on the "long ton" (2240 lbs.) but were paid on the "short ton" (2000 lbs.) In other words, for every ton loaded, 240 pounds were loaded for free.
- They were not paid on time (i.e., by the hour) but on tonnage. This means they were not paid for

setting roof timbers, laying track for the coal cars, removing ground water that commonly seeps into a mine, or any of the other numerous activities required to mine coal. Even the trip through the mine to the face of the coal – which could easily be as far as two miles into the mountain – and their trip back out of the mine at the end of the day (whether on foot or by man trip) were done for free. Simply put, they were paid *only* for the coal they loaded and none of the other mining tasks.

- They had to pay the company for the tools required to do their work. They even had to pay to have their picks sharpened.
- The company had exclusive control of the weighing system. This is crucial because this meant they could declare any amount of a load of coal to be unusable rock, slate, or shale that they wanted to – whether true or not. Thus, the miner's weight of coal was lowered by that amount and consequently, his pay. There is no telling how much money was stolen from miners through this method.

Under such a greedy and subservient system, it is no wonder that the miners finally got fed up.

The tension had been building for months and collectively the miners decided they had taken all the mistreatment they could stomach. On May 5, 1931, it all came to a head in Evarts.

Dad (fourteen years old at the time) and a friend, Bus Owens, had spring fever on that bright Tuesday and decided it was too fine a day to spend in school. They took the side door out of the second floor of the old Evarts school and headed up the tracks.

When we got past Draper we went up in that holler where Doc Lewis lived. On this side of the graveyard and on up in there they was an apple orchard and an old farmhouse. And me and Bus went up there and was a-eatin' apples and we come back down out of there 'bout the time for school to break. [A smart practice if you were playing hooky!] We took off down that hill from Doc Lewis's then, a-goin' to Draper.

We got down to the road and was walkin' it before we went down the Draper hill – we was still on the highway there – and that's where that gang of men, company gun thugs and them, was a-walkin'. They'd got out of their cars, you see. They had left their cars back up the road.

They was a-walkin' in front of us. We follered 'em down that hill. They got down there at the railroad track that was in front of Draper tipple, and we'd notice they'd walk and look over at the tipple a-skittish [nervous] like. They'd keep lookin' around.

When they got to the railroad track, then they took up it. They was a-headin' toward Evarts. It wasn't too long then, buddy, til the shootin' started!

Me and Bus didn't know they was gun thugs, you see. We did know they had guns, for we could see 'em, but we didn't know who they was. We was just layin' back and a-follerin' them to see what they was up to. We kept back a little ways 'cause we knew somethin' was up for they had guns.

They'd stop ever so often and look over at the Draper tipple as they was a-walkin'. They was afraid that somebody was goin' to see them. The tipple set down there right up close to the railroad.

We are traveling through the very spot where this all occurred on one of our information-gathering trips to Harlan County. We pull over to the side of the road and I say, "So this is where it happened, Dad?" He continues:

Yeah, yeah. Right here. Right here [he points] is where they found a piece of one of the gun thug's skull. A colored miner had shot him and he picked that piece of his skull up off of the track. He said, 'I'm gonna make me a whit rock out of it.' That man, that gun thug, was a mean one they said. That colored miner got him though. [The name of that "gun thug" is known to me, but out of respect for his kin, I have not named him. I will say, however, that he was known as "the Kaiser,"[22] and that he was reported to be "the most hated Harlan mine guard" of all – and that is saying something.] These guys the operators hired was nothin' but gun thugs but of course the coal companies saw to it that they was 'deputized.' That's why I say they ain't nothin' worse than dirty law, buddy.

I walked the ditch where they laid after the shootin'. You could see the blood and brains and such. It was in the ditch line there at Aunt Josie Middleton's [not his aunt, this is how she was known by the locals], you know, going below the bell crossing. The miners were over here to the right [he points], down below that dirt bank there.

They was a-shootin' up at the highway at them gun thugs.

On one of the trips to Harlan County we stopped at 30 Camp to talk to Joe Asbury, an old friend to Mother and Dad and an old miner. Mr. Asbury was a fine man and a trove of information.

I share the following dialogue between Dad and Mr. Asbury because I enjoyed so much the experience of hearing two old miners from a bygone era share some time together and reminisce. Dad loved that visit. He was talking to someone from his world. He would refer to that visit with Mr. Asbury time and again in the years ahead.

I ask Mr. Asbury if he lived in Harlan County during the Battle of Evarts.

"No, I wasn't here then. That happened before I come over here."

Dad remarks, "I remember, Joe, being right there. I was at the spot where they shot --- --- and them, layin' in the ditch line there at Aunt Josie Middleton's, you know, goin' below the bell crossing."

"Josie told me all about that battle. You know, I used to have a picture of that old house there somewhere, the one that got shot up at the bell crossing," says Mr. Asbury.

Dad replies: "I lived in that house after that, Joe! I told Mike, I've dug bullets out of that house, out of the lower end there, where it was shot up from the battle. I never will forget seein' them holes and rememberin' bein' right there with Bus when all of that happened."[This is the very house Dad and his parents lived in briefly, before moving to Bailey Creek.]

Figure 5. The bell crossing house in Evarts.

Dad goes on:

"I was tellin' Mike a story about when I was a kid at Draper and Aunt Josie Middleton. I used to do yard work and such for her ever once in a while when I was a young'n. Well, it was gettin' close to dinner time and Josie said to me, 'Carl, do you want to eat with us? We're having fried chicken.' Well, I jumped on that, buddy! I eat so much of that fried chicken I was embarrassed 'cause I had so many bones on my plate. I got to sneakin' and puttin' them bones in my pocket so I could throw them away. I went out of there with a pocket full of chicken bones!

I told Mike I wish I could better recall about 50 years back. Then I could help him more."

Mr. Asbury responds, "Well, there's some things you'd want to call back and then some things you wouldn't."

"Well, that's right, Joe. It shore is," says Dad.

Mr. Asbury continues, "My family is all dead, Carl. We buried my younger sister in February of '92, and then we buried my other sister in August of '92. And that's all of them but me."

"Well, I'm the only one that's left of mine," Dad replies.

"Is that right?" asks Mr. Asbury. "There's people buried up in these hills [30] and up at 31, I don't know at 'em. They'd know tales, wouldn't they! I remember way back there going to a funeral for, oh, what's his name, let me think. He was a Smith, and the weather was awful!"

Dad jumps in:

"Oh yeah buddy, I know the one you're talkin' about! It was Sine Smith's dad. Me and Elmer Martin was pallbearers for that funeral. We went back to 31 tipple and we had to build a fire to get warm. We stood around that fire because it was a-sleetin' and a-rainin' on us fierce. I tell you what, it was the worst weather for a funeral I'd ever seen and I've seen a lot of 'em!"

"That's right. It was Sine's dad. You know, I talked to Sine on Saturday night and his dad died later that night," says Mr. Asbury.

I say to him, "You knew Sine?"

"Oh yeah!," he exclaims. "He was the best feller I was ever acquainted with."

The ending of that conversation is tender to me because Sine Smith was my uncle. He was married to my mother's younger sister, Dollie. (Dollie had divorced J. T. Latham some years earlier over his infidelity. She later married Sine Smith. In fact, it was Dad who introduced Sine to Dollie. After his Army service in WWII, Sine came back to Black Mountain and to mining. Dad introduced him to Dollie in the hope that they would hit it off and eventually marry. He wanted Dollie to marry Sine because he was such a good man.) Sine died on August 31, 1968, from a cancer that was as insidious as it was aggressive. He was four days past his fifty-sixth birthday.

As one who knew Sine family-close, I can echo Mr. Asbury's sentiments. Sine Harlan Smith was the finest, gentlest man I have ever known. Any member of our family would tell you exactly the same. It was a privilege to be his nephew.

Figure 6. Sine Harlan Smith

The Coxton years comprised the most intense period of the labor strife in Dad's story. These were dangerous years. "Many times when I'd tell Della bye in the mornin', I didn't know if I'd ever see her again."

These were years of pickets and picket lines, of "gun thugs" and power abuse, of vigilantism and reckonings. They were austere, dark times. There was little gray to be found and on both sides of the issue the mindset was "you're either for us or against us." The following story illustrates this point.

One of the areas the organizers and miners sought to unionize was the mine of Benham (owned by International Harvester), near Lynch (owned by U.S. Coal and Coke, a subsidiary of U.S. Steel – all the coal mined at Lynch went to the Gary, Indiana, plant of U. S. Steel). Benham was a large mine (nearly 700 miners at its peak) but Lynch was a massive mining operation. In fact, Lynch was the largest operation in Harlan County (peaking at nearly 1,700 miners). Benham and Lynch[23] were sights of some intense picketing. (Lynch became a union mine in 1937.)

> We went over there one night, I went with Floyd Tippet. [Mother jumps in here to describe Mr. Tippet as being "like Carl."] He had a .45 automatic and I had a .45 automatic. We was going up the old road above Rosspoint.

> Well, --- --- [Again, I am withholding the name here] run a gas station up there. He was a gun thug for the mines of Benham and Lynch. He operated all over Harlan County, though.

> I told Floyd, 'give me yours.' I knocked the safety off of his and off mine too. It was two .45s I had then. I had his in my left hand and mine in the

right. If that feller had been outside, I was goin' to empty both of 'em at him, buddy. He was known to knock miners around and pistol whip 'em when he had the drop on one or had him outnumbered. If he'd been out there he wouldn't a-been doin' no more knockin' around.

Absolutely stunned by this, Mother remarked, "I never heard that one." To which Dad replied, "Well, you didn't know about...I didn't want you to know, honey."

Mother, a gentler soul you'll never meet said, "Why would you shoot a man that hadn't done anything to you?" She just couldn't get her head around this. Similarly, Dad couldn't understand why such a question was even asked, or why the answer wasn't obvious.

"Cause he was on the other side, honey! He was one of the thugs in their clan who'd been visitin' violence on miners and we knowed it. We all knowed it!"

It's no doubt hard for the modern reader to understand this, especially if you aren't "from around here," as the saying goes. But such was the climate of the times.

And it was most certainly not a one-sided attitude. Dad tells of a regrettable night when a car of company "deputies" drove through one of the camps – "it was up there like you was goin' to Shields or Highsplint, on the left up there" – and strafed the house of a known union organizer with machine gun fire. The house was shot up and one of the miner's children, his young daughter, was killed. No arrests were made.

Mother recalls a similar story of her own which occurred around the same time as the Battle of Evarts. A classmate, Ralph Nolan, was killed when gunmen for the operators fired blindly into the home. They were intending to murder young Ralph's father and instead killed the son. As Mother recalls, she and the murdered child, Ralph Nolan, were in the seventh grade at the time. Unlike the miners, company "deputies" were known for being indiscriminate and indifferent in their targeting.

One cannot address the tension that existed in Harlan County between coal operators and miners in the early to mid-twentieth century without looking briefly at the county government of the time. The miner-operator conflict did not occur in a vacuum. In fact, it is doubtful that the conflict could have become so "bloody" or lasted so long, were it not for the relationship that existed between the coal operators and local government (and to be more accurate, even state and federal government).

The partnership that existed between county government and the coal operators in Harlan County in the first half of the twentieth century leaves one incredulous. To merely call it collusion in no way captures the extent of the matter. The relationship could be more accurately described as nothing short of political and commercial incest. And it was rampant. It is little wonder that in 1936, John Y. Brown, Speaker of the House of the Kentucky Legislature took as his subject for his radio broadcast decrying the conditions in Harlan County, "The Feudal Lords of Harlan."[24]

To report on conditions existing in Harlan County at that time, then Governor Ruby Laffoon commissioned an investigatory team in 1935, headed by Adjutant General Henry Denhardt. In my own words, I have pulled the following points from the narrative of the commission's findings. (All comments within quotes are the actual wording of the report.)

- A group of coal mine operators colluding with certain public officials have financed a near "reign of terror" in Harlan County.
- This terror is aimed at the coal miners and their families, and union organizers.
- This reality creates a "monster-like reign of oppression" which strikes to the heart of Harlan County's social structure.
- There is virtually no tolerance of free speech and the right to assemble peacefully in Harlan County. [The Knoxville *News Sentinel* observed at the time, "It seems like the old feudal system argument that the slave can have nothing to say as to his master's treatment of him."[25]]
- The cause of these injustices appears to be the desire of the mine owners to accumulate vast fortunes for themselves via the oppression of the miners.
- The chief tool of the mine owners/operators is the sheriff's office.
- Statements by miners favorable to the union or the attendance of union meetings result in termination of job and eviction from company housing.
- Many miners and organizers are being assaulted and otherwise mistreated by so-called "peace officers" hired by certain operators.
- It is beyond question that Harlan County's Sheriff Middleton uses his cohorts to carry out his own ends and that he is in league with the operators.
- Mine guards should not be used off mining property. The use of gunmen and those with criminal records as guards or deputies must cease.

- Mine guards should not form "flying squadrons" to intimidate and terrorize people county-wide at the sheriff's behest.
- Acts of terrorism used by the minions of the owners/operators include strafing the homes of miners and organizers with gunfire and dynamiting their homes.
- The unilateral enforcement of the law (in favor of the owner/operators) must cease and the deputizing of mine guards must be abolished.[26]

Sheriff John Henry Blair (1930-1933) openly demonstrated the reality of just what the miners faced as far as the law was concerned when he brazenly stated, "I did all in my power to aid the coal operators."[27] Little wonder that a 1931 Kentucky state investigatory commission reported that the sheriff's office meted out the law "in a lawless manner, in Harlan County."[28]

Ask any old Harlan County miner or miner's wife about the Harlan County sheriffs back then. Or get a feel for the times by reading the famous poem "Which Side Are You On," written in 1931 – the year of the Battle of Evarts – by Florence Reece. Mrs. Reece was not only the daughter of a Harlan County miner, she was also the wife of a union organizer.

The story is this: Sam Reece (Florence's husband) was a miner and union organizer. As such, he was a marked man. Receiving word one night that Sheriff Blair and some "deputies" were coming for him, he quickly left the house. Mr. Reece assumed this would cool the sheriff's heels. He was wrong. Later that evening, Blair and his men showed up at the house looking for him. Mrs. Reece and their seven children were there alone. She boldly says to the sheriff, "What are you here for? You know there's nothing but a lot of little hungry children here."[29] Without a search warrant or any other legal right, the sheriff and his minions searched the house thoroughly and, not finding Mr. Reece, they set a clandestine watch outside the house with the suspected intent of gunning Sam down if he had returned.

This affair did not sit well with the miner's wife. So incensed was Mrs. Reece by this malicious intrusion that she jerked a page off the wall calendar and angrily composed the now-famous poem, "Which Side Are You On?" She turned the poem to song, singing it to the tune of the old hymn, *Lay the Lily Low.*[30]

Figure 7. Grave of J. H. Blair

The attempt to break and subdue the thousands of miners in Harlan County called for a great amount of force on behalf of the operators and the county law. To address this, the presiding sheriff would swell the ranks of his force. In 1937, for example, Sheriff Theodore

Middleton had 163 subordinates working for him. Tellingly, these men were not paid through proper legal channels, that is, from the coffers of the county government. In fact, of these 163 men, only three of them were paid from legitimate county funds.[31] Instead, they were hired by the coal companies to work hand-in-hand with the local law. In reality, this meant they worked only for the coal companies, as the law was in the coal companies' back pocket. Another example, of the 169 men hired by Sheriff Blair, all but six were reportedly paid by the coal operators.[32]

To put a skein of laughable credibility on it all, these men were "deputized" to legalize their behavior. As absurd as it is, some of these men were actually coal company officials. Some of the rest of the "deputies" were local men, while still others were brought in from the outside. Character was apparently not a part of the job description for these positions. Many of the men possessed a well-established dark reputation and more than a few even had criminal records, including felonies. To illustrate, of the 169 new hires of Sheriff Blair mentioned above, sixty-four of the men had been indicted and thirty-four were convicted felons. One "deputy," Bill Randolph, was in jail on a murder charge – his fourth – when Harlan operators secured his release by paying the bond, and then hired him as a "guard" at Three Point.[33] On June 11, 1931, Randolph reportedly shot and killed miner John Casteen in Cawood. He was soon cleared of the charge.

Chicago seems to have been a preferred source for the men brought in from the outside. When news correspondent Boris Israel was grabbed by "deputies," (ironically, on the steps of the Harlan Courthouse) driven to a secluded road, thrown from the car and shot, one journalist described it as being done "in perfect Chicago style."[34]

Harlan County government was a viper's den in those days. Here are four – and they represent but a few – examples of how Harlan County carried on around election time:

- The county's entire gubernatorial vote of 1931 was rendered void because of inconsistencies in the voting at the Verda coal camp (owned by Harlan-Wallins Coal Corporation).
- During Kentucky's next gubernatorial election, presiding Governor Lafoon sent the National Guard to Harlan to thwart a suspected attempt to corrupt the election. *He had to do this three times.*
- In 1937, a specially appointed circuit court judge invalidated the county's election for sheriff, county attorney, coroner, and jailor because of corrupt practices within both political parties.
- In the 1942 United States Senate elections, a federal district court convicted forty-four county election officials of fraud.[35]

This is, of course, not to say there were no honest government officials in play in the Harlan County government of those days. However, evidence is indisputable to say that if you were on the legitimate Harlan County payroll and you were honest and upright, you were a glaring standout among your peers. In fact, if a duly elected official (as opposed to those owned by the coal companies) was an honest man, he was in danger of encountering the fate of County

Attorney Elmon Middleton. Attorney Middleton was most unusual in that he was deemed by the miners of Harlan County to be a fair man. In 1935 he was killed by a car bomb. The bomb the killer or killers made was sufficiently powerful to blow part of his engine a quarter of a mile from the blast site.[36] The apparent motive for his targeting and murder was attributed to the fact that he was trying to eradicate fraud and corruption from Harlan County government.[37]

This is the kind of response anyone could expect if they dared to take on the system. The collusion between the coal operators and county government brooked no opposition. And the above story goes to show that even being a respected duly-elected public official did not take you out of harm's way if you challenged the status quo.

What chance did the miners have in a system where local sheriffs openly voiced and demonstrated their allegiance and indebtedness to the county's only industrial monopoly? Where the county sheriff owned stock in at least three coal companies and sold supplies to six company stores from his own dairy farm?[38] Where coal companies owned and operated the local police force? What kind of justice could they expect in a county where the wife of a sitting judge was part owner of a coal company, and the county prosecuting attorney was on retainer to three of the largest coal operations in the county?[39] With all of the tremendous power behind the corrupt county officials and the coal operators in that day, it is little wonder that the miners felt they had no choice but to fight back. And fight they did, any way they could. Their only weapon of impact, however, was the organized strike.

Figure 8. Evidence of the miners' only real weapon – empty coal cars during the strike in 1939 in Harlan County. (Courtesy Harlan County Mine Strike Photographic Collection, 81PA109, Special Collections, University of Kentucky. Used by permission.)

There were two terms thrown about in those days, and to be called either was about the worst label a man could have. The first has been referenced a number of times already and we have just discussed them as being "deputies." But that's not the term. Miners never called these men deputies. To them, to do so was an insult to the concept of true law officers everywhere. To the miners and their families everywhere these men were known by the derisive term "gun thugs." They were despised men to the miners, their families, and to union organizers. The "gun thugs" were the enemy who, as demonstrated above, were bought and paid for by the coal operators.

Figure 9. Mine "gun thugs" at a picket site in Harlan County. (Courtesy Dave Johnson at homestead.com. Used by permission.)

The second term belongs on the other side of the fray – on the miners' side. In many ways, this name was more despicable to the majority of miners than was "gun thug." To his dying day, just the mention of the term would raise Dad's ire. The word, of course, is "scab."

A scab was an ostracized man, a man without a country. The scab didn't want his life or his family jeopardized (as if any miner did). He didn't want the struggle and conflict. He wanted to cross the picket line and continue to work. (Though the union men would say of them, "They shore didn't mind getting the advantages we fought and died for though!")

The "scab" has been the recipient of derision for as many years as there have been picket lines to cross.

One writer dipped his pen in acid and wrote the following:

> When a scab comes down the street, men turn their backs, angels weep in heaven, and the Devil shuts the gates of Hell to keep him out...Judas Iscariot was a gentleman compared to a scab. For betraying his master, he had character enough to hang himself. A scab has not.[40]

The tension between the union miners and the scabs was close in intensity to that existing with the operators of nonunion mines and their gun thugs. Dad says, "Lots of them that wouldn't go on picket lines and support efforts to unionize would get throwed off the nearest bridge and into the river [by union miners]." This wasn't intended to kill or maim any miner, and didn't. It was done to send a message and for humiliation.

Figure 10. National Guard troops escorting "scab" miners during the 1939 strike. (Courtesy Harlan County Mine Strike Photographic Collection, 81PA109, Special Collections, University of Kentucky. Used by Permission.)

81

The strains in relationships caused among these groups: operators, gun thugs, scabs, union miners and union organizers, lasted for decades, for generations, and even existed within families. To this day, wounds are not totally healed in those hills. And though their numbers grow fewer by the year, people still remember. Scars last a lot longer than the wounds which caused them.

In the majority, the Coxton years were about working hard to mine coal and working hard to organize nonunion mines. I asked Dad if he could recall the worst picketing experience he ever had:

When we went to Three Point,[41] honey. It's up in a holler off to the right, just before you get to Cawood.

We come out of there that evening, after picketing there that day. You had to come out through a tunnel up there to get out. We had been picketing and the state troopers were up there. It had been a peaceful picket, as pickets go. The troopers let us out but they intended not to let other picketers get in, you see, even though picketing is legal. When we come out of the holler, down through that tunnel, the state troopers was set up there and they intended that nobody else would get in to picket once we got out.

We just doubled back and come up another fork and we crossed one little ol' branch I guess a dozen times a-zigzaggin' around, a-goin' back across that mountain in the night. Man, that was a long haul! We climbed up to the top of the mountain and crossed over and come down in there til [so] we'd be there the next mornin' when they went to work, you see.

What made it so hairy was that if the gun thugs had been roamin' about they'd of just cut us to pieces. We wouldn't a-stood a chance because we didn't all have guns or nothin'. We was just picketing. And the state troopers were there too and, buddy, they shore wouldn't have helped us!

I said I asked Dad for his worst picketing experience, but that is not quite accurate. In actuality, I was asking him for his second-worst picketing experience. I already knew the worst one. All three of us sitting around the kitchen table that afternoon knew the worst one. We knew instinctively that it wasn't included in the question. Dad called it the saddest day of his life.

Coal-yard Facts

More than 90% of the coal mined in the U. S. is purchased by utility companies.

CHAPTER 6

In Coal Blood

It's April 2, 1941, and there's a nip in the spring air this Wednesday morning. Times are tense. The union miners are turning up the pressure on nonunion mines by increasing their picketing. The nonunion operators have their backs up and are ready for a fight. Tensions have been hardened in stone since many months earlier (specifically, May, 1939), when the Governor at that time, Albert B. "Happy" Chandler,[42] sent 850 National Guardsmen in on behalf of the coal operators. (Here is another example. Eight years earlier, two days after the Battle of Evarts, then Governor Sampson sent in 325 National Guardsmen and the miners were elated. Scores of miners met them waving American flags. The Guard arrived, combat gear on, with their machine guns, grenades, and an armored tank to rein in the "gun thugs" and bring a sense of order and justice to their plight – or so the miners thought. They soon learned different. Lt. Col. Sydney Smith, who was in charge of the National Guard contingency on site said, "These damned miners thought we came here to help them."[43])

Figure 11. National Guardsmen setting up a machine gun position on a hillside against picketing miners on the road below. (Courtesy Harlan County Mine Strike Photographic Collection, 81PA109, Special Collections, Univ. of Kentucky. Used by permission.)

Happy Chandler had sent them in by railroad cars, you know, like the people lived in that done work on the railroad. He sent them in to keep down trouble, to try to keep us – see, back then everybody dreaded the Black Mountain group. We wouldn't call each other by name, we just called ourselves the Jones boys. [I often wonder if this was a nod to the famous labor organizer Mary Harris "Mother" Jones. Mother Jones was known as the "Miners' Angel." There is an impressive monument dedicated to her in the Union Miners Cemetery in Mt. Olive, Illinois.] We didn't want them to know our names for they'd target your home or your family, you see. They didn't have no scruples. They didn't care, buddy. [And as history clearly bears out, the man of little character has weapons and tactics at his disposal that a man of integrity will not touch.[44]]

Figure 12. Standoff between picketing miners and the National Guard.
(Courtesy Harlan County Mine Strike Photographic Collection,
81PA109, Special Collections, Univ. of Kentucky. Used by permission.)

We'd come to a picket line and we'd tell 'em [nonunion miners and/or scabs] we didn't want to have to make the trip back up there, and that if we did, it'd be different the next time. Most of 'em would say, 'Well, you won't have to make another trip back. We just won't do it [i.e., won't go to work].'

That April day was to be a day of picketing like many before – a day of vitriol and posturing, a day of threats and counter threats on both sides. But it would not be a typical day, not typical at all.

The day began early, as a miner's day always did. The Jones boys, miners from other union mines, and union organizers had been to the nonunion Kitts mine (Clover Fork Coal Company) before breakfast to picket. The men picketed for a couple of hours, then left Kitts. Dad asked his brother Chalk, who also had been at the Kitts picket, to return home to Coxton with him and join him for breakfast. Chalk was the brother nearest to Dad in both age and affection. They were very much alike and they were oh-so close. Chalk lived further up the road past Evarts, in New Camp, with his wife Rosa and their four children. As Coxton was closer to Kitts than New Camp, Dad asking him back to the house for breakfast made practical sense. Dad recalls:

Figure 13. Charles "Chalk" Ruth

I tried to get Chalk to go home to eat breakfast with me but he already had plans. Me, Floyd Tippit, and J. T. Latham went back to Coxton to eat our breakfast. Floyd went on to his house and J. T. come home with me to eat breakfast with me and Della. We was to all meet after that in Harlan then, on 1st Street, there by the courthouse.

We was to meet there and then we was going to Mary Helen,[45] to picket. [Mary Helen mine was off to the left up in a hollow just before Cawood, as one is travelling from Harlan. It was not far from the aforementioned Chevrolet mine.] We was goin' to Mary Helen for a while and then we was goin' to Crummies Creek to picket there at that mine. We planned to be through picketing Mary Helen and Crummies Creek by about dinner [lunch] time or just after.

I asked Dad if anything of significance had happened at the Mary Helen picket. He recalls a physical altercation which occurred with a "scab" miner:

They [some picketers] run a guy around down the hill and he got trapped by a fence. They hit him and throwed him down. And they was beatin' him up and I come over and stopped them. I said, 'You've done enough damage. Leave him alone.'

Come to find out, when I got closer, I knowed him! It was --- --- [name omitted]. Him and his brother used to work at Draper with me when I first started mining. I set down with him and he told me, he said, 'Carl, I've been a union man a long time,' or something like that. I said, 'Well ---, I guess a leopard can change his spots.' I said, 'Well, if you are, you ain't got nothin' to worry about, buddy.'

Having ended their picket of Mary Helen for the day, the miners then head down to Crummies Creek [Crummies Creek mine lay along old Highway 421, and was also near Cawood] to picket there. They park their cars just shy of where the track crosses the highway, parallel with the track running to Crummies Creek mine. The picketers pull their vehicles off to the side of the road in a sort of ditch. Parking here means they are not trespassing on company property, which is against the law. The tipple is off to the right just back a ways. The company store is on the other side of the crossing track and off to the right.

Some of the men want to get a bottle of pop and a snack cake or a sandwich before they set up the picket line. They walk across the tracks, through the store parking lot, up the eight steps to the porch, and go inside.

As Dad is recounting this story, we are sitting on the very spot where the miners parked that day. In the vehicle are Dad, Mother, my sister Sandra (who lived in Harlan at that time and was with us on this occasion) and I. I remember sitting there and seeing the events unfold in my mind's eye, as Dad walked us through what transpired. I still recall the melancholy feeling I experienced that day, as Dad spoke:

When we left Mary Helen, we pulled our cars alongside the road, just short of the railroad crossing. We was on the side of the tracks where the tipple was. Just across the tracks from where we're sittin' now was the company store on the right there. [From where we were sitting, we were looking directly at the building that had housed the company store. A private business was in the building at that time.]

The miner drivin' the sound car [a car with loudspeakers mounted on top of it] got on the speakers and said to be sure we didn't block the road in any way with our cars. We never did that. He was just bein' careful. We was always careful settin' up a picket not to do nothin' to break the law for that would have played right into their hands.

There was a good many of us,[46] but I couldn't guess how many, now. It's been too long. There was the Jones boys [Black Mountain miners] and miners from the other union mines, and organizers. We was just a-millin' about, a-talkin' about how we was gonna set up our picket line. Some of 'em had walked down to the company store to get a bottle of pop and a bite of somethin' to eat. It was before dinner [lunch] time.

I heard a ruckus and looked up and a miner had got into it on the porch of the store with a scab miner. The scab was a colored feller. I don't know who jumped who. I was standing by the sound car and had my foot up on the bumper. I took my foot down and was about to head over to the fight to see what was goin' on.

All of a sudden, it sounded to me like we was in a war! Bullets was flyin' all around us. They was a cloud around us where bullets was hittin' dirt and the blacktop [road – old Highway 421].

They had a machine gun set up on the mountain there behind the store and one set up on the mountain there across the road [he points]. They was a vent up in the gable of the company store there – them four windows weren't there then – and they was a machine gun there too, or a B.A.R. [The Browning Automatic Rifle is a machine gun-type military weapon].[47]

Mary Helen had called them to let them know we was likely headed there to picket. They was a-waitin' for us, buddy.

Figure 14. Crummies Creek Company Store. Tragically, the building has now been razed.

The miners had gone to Crummies Creek just to picket. They no doubt expected to swap a lot of angry verbal jabs with the "deputies" and "scabs," a common occurrence at pickets. They gave as well as they got when that happened. However, they weren't at all ready for what they ran into, nor were they prepared for it. Some of the miners had a pistol in their pocket but in the Harlan County of that era, this was not even noteworthy. Dad had nothing but his three-blade Hen & Rooster pocket knife. Hardly a weapon.

These miners were mountain men. They were as wise as serpents and as cunning as foxes in matters like this.

There is no way they go into that scene unarmed and walking about in the open, much less go into the opposing side's company store to buy a snack, had they been looking for or expecting a fight. No way. They were sitting ducks.

The opposition knew exactly what they were doing. In military terms, they had triangulated their target and they had control of the high ground. The place was a killing field.

They shot a lead mine around the sound car where I was standing. Miners were callin' out to take cover and took to runnin'. Miners was a-jumpin' into a ditch that was right here [the ditch has since been filled in], and runnin' back toward the gons [train coal cars – "gon" is short for "gondola car"] that was on the tipple track.

I walked back toward the gons to get cover. We knowed if we could get between them gons they couldn't see us, and if they couldn't see us, they couldn't shoot us. I remember seeing one feller, a miner, put an arm up over the end of a gon to rest his shootin' hand on. He had a long-barrel pistol. I'll never forget it. He had a long-barrel pistol and he was a-shootin' back at the thug with the machine gun up in the gable of the store.

The state troopers then come up about that time. We was in the ditch and back down across the track among the gons. I can still remember seeing their [troopers'] cars there. I went to them and said, 'Why don't you go up there and stop them damn guys from murderin'! They're just ambushin' our fellers! They're just bushwhackin' us!'

One of 'em [Likely, Colonel Nelson, of the Kentucky State Police, himself. See below.] said, mockin' like, 'We ain't got no rights across that crossing.'

I said back, 'Well, it's a funny damn thing to me.' I said, 'If it was us a-doin' the damage you'd take the right and the authority!'

(Dad's comments here fit precisely with the report of the incident in the *Harlan Daily Enterprise* on that day which stated, "...Colonel Nelson, Chief of the Kentucky State Highway Patrol 'looked on' conditions of the county along with several car loads of state police. Colonel Nelson declared that he was merely observing conditions..." Carnage of this scale – the worst since the Battle of Evarts ten years earlier and one in which one side is being ambushed by the other – is underway and the Kentucky State Police, led by their Colonel, are merely "observing conditions?!")

I asked Dad where he first ran to for safety. "I didn't run, honey. I just turned from the sound car and walked down to the gons and got between two of 'em."

That might sound hard to believe, for the reader. It might sound like a bit of embellished bravado. I assure you, that's not the case. Dad was the calmest man in a crisis I have ever seen. Anybody who knew Carl Ruth would tell you that such a response would be exactly how he would act in this melee. In my entire life, I never saw Dad in any situation in which he manifested fear or panic, nor knew anyone or anything he was afraid of. (With one exception. Dad was afraid of dogs. He was terrified of them, in fact. He was bitten rather viciously by a dog when he was a small boy, and that experience marked him for life.)

But there was something else at work here besides calm courage. Incredulous, I asked Dad why he didn't run for his life like all the other miners were naturally and sensibly doing.

> I just didn't. I don't know, Mike. I just don't care. It's a wonder they didn't kill me and I know that. I know that full well. I don't know what's wrong with me, Mike. Nothin' like that don't scare me. And it didn't scare me then. I didn't run like them other fellers. I just turned and walked on down through there. It's a wonder they hadn't killed me. The Lord was just lookin' after me by some means, and I know it! I mean, they had shot up a lead mines around me. There was a cloud like where they was plowin' up dirt and the blacktop all around me with bullets.

The shooting lasted for several minutes. After the mayhem, most of the miners, now furious over the ambush, were ready for blood. Some said they were going back to Harlan and elsewhere to get weapons, and then coming back. Others, feeling lucky to have survived such a maelstrom, just hurriedly left for the haven of home.

> After the shootin', we came back out from between and behind the gons. We was walking back up to the crossin' to get back in our cars to leave, you see.
>
> I saw Ross, Ross Hensley, he was one of Dewey Hensley's boys. I said, 'Ross, have you seen Chalk?' And he said, 'I think he's gone to Harlan with some of 'em to get some guns, Carl.' That's what Ross told me.

Interestingly, Dad's oldest brother, Lawrence, was also there. He too was a Black Mountain miner. But

Dad says it didn't occur to him to ask about Lawrence. [Their brother Ed was another of the Ruth brothers who mined at Black Mountain, but Dad cannot recall if Ed was on the pickets that day or not.] It wasn't that Dad didn't love Lawrence. He and Chalk were just so very close – two peas in the proverbial pod.

I then run into Lawrence. I shore was relieved to see him. Me and Lawrence, and J. T. Latham got in a car and took off to Harlan. We knowed some miners had been shot for we seen it. And too, the ambulances had passed us as we was a-headin' to Harlan. And some of our fellers had some of the wounded in their cars. They was a-flyin' past us to get to the hospital. We was goin' to the hospital to see who had been shot. I was wantin' to know if Chalk was there.

We parked on the street and went into the Harlan Hospital there on Mound Street. We went around to the back of the hospital to that entrance and a nurse was standin' there. I knowed her. It was Lawrence Tony's wife and she was a nurse there. Her name was Elsie, Elsie or Sylvia, I can't remember now which, but I think it was Elsie. Her last name was Tony. She was kindly [kind of] redheaded. She knew me and I says 'Elsie, is Chalk in there.'

She said, 'No, Carl. We got a number of them in there but Chalk's not one of them. He may be at the undertaker's office. We heard they took some down there to Cawood's [Cumberland Hardware Morgue].' I'll never forget her sayin' that.

Well, me, Lawrence, and J. T. went down there to Cawood's. It was there close to the old Margie Grand Theater, across from that Doughboy statue in front of the courthouse. The undertaker's was above the hardware store. The hardware was on the first floor and the second floor was the undertaker's. They was an elevator up to the undertaker's.

> Well, we went down the alley in back of the building, you see. We come in the door and over here [he illustrates with his hand] was the elevator. We stepped on the elevator to go up to the undertaker's and right over here [his voice cracks] laid Chalk's black hat on a box. I knowed then them murderers at Crummies had got him.

To clarify, I asked Dad if he was saying that Chalk's hat was in the elevator.

"Yeah." [He says lowly and despondently, seeing that hat again in his mind.]

"You rode up the elevator with his hat?"

"Yeah. But I left it a-layin' there. I didn't pick it up or nothin'. I couldn't bring myself to even touch it."

Black hat, black day.

> Well, we got in the room there and they had Chalk's body a-layin' on the table. Lord have mercy, it tore me all to pieces when I seen him a-layin' there.

> The undertaker said, 'Carl, there's one thing you don't have to worry about. He didn't suffer.' He said one of the shots broke his neck. He said, 'He didn't suffer, for it killed him instantly.' I said, 'Well, thank the Lord for that.'

I asked Dad if he could bear to look at his brother. (I asked this because I had long known that one of Uncle Chalk's entry wounds was particularly diabolical. Specifically, he had been shot in the back of the head. Out of concern for Dad, I did not broach this fact at the time.) "Yeah, I did, honey," says Dad in a quiet and slow voice, no doubt reliving the moment. "I looked at him real good." He continues:

Chalk was a-layin' on the undertaker's table. The bullet hole [entrance wound] was in the back of his head and it had blowed out just under his cheek. I don't remember which side for it tore me up so. It was a mess. [For the record, the bullet had entered on the left side of the back of the head and exited just under the right cheek.]

They had two other miners that had been killed[48] at Crummies in that room too. A colored miner, he was from 31 too, named Ed Tye had been murdered and Virgil Hampton. Virgil was a union organizer. [Another miner will soon be there. Oscar Goodlin, a miner from Lynch, is in the hospital, just minutes away from death.]

Virgil had been a field worker for the UMWA. He might have been a miner too, I can't recall. All three of them was a-layin' in there shot up and dead. [As fate would have it, Virgil Hampton was the son of the Mrs. Hampton Mother and Dad had briefly lived above in Coxton.] They was several other miners that had been wounded, but they was at the hospital.

Mother later told me more about the scene which had taken place in the undertaker's prep room that day. She had waited until she could tell me this alone, so Dad would not hear it:

J. T. [Latham] told me that he liked to never got Carl away from Chalk's body. He was holding on to his brother and wouldn't let go of him. J. T. told me that while Carl was clinging to Chalk he just kept saying 'I promise you that I will neither eat, nor drink, nor sleep til I get the man that done this!'

That is how J. T. told it to Mother. Out of respect for Mother, he cleaned the story up a bit. What Dad actually said, I know because he had told me this earlier, was not as delicate. What he said is "...til I get the sonofabitch that done this!"

This fits with what Dad later told me. I asked him if he thought he was in shock when he was there in Cawood's. "No, huh-uh, no. I wasn't in shock. I was mad!"

News of the carnage spread fast, by radio and by word of mouth. Families all over Harlan County were worried sick that their husband, their son, their father or brother was among the wounded or dead.

From Mother's own experience:

> Word spread that there had been killings. We heard that they had machine-gunned the miners. One of the miners who had been at Crummies came back to Coxton and told us. I didn't know if Carl was alive or not; we didn't know who was killed yet.
>
> I knew, of course, Carl was there and I was worried sick. I was worried about Chalk and Lawrence too because I knew they were there. I don't remember if Ed was or not.
>
> It's funny. I had just left Lawrence's house[49] and gone back home. I had been visiting Lela [Uncle Lawrence's wife] for a little bit. They lived in Coxton too, on the hill up behind the company store. I was back home though when the news broke.

That was the first of two trips Mother would make to see Lela that day. The second was unplanned. "When I got the news, I ran up the back alley to tell Lela there had been trouble. I told her I didn't know if family had been hurt or killed, or not."

Dad breaks in here and adds an adjunct to the story:

When Ervin [second eldest brother], they said when Ervin got the news he said, 'Lord have mercy – they've killed my baby brother.' He thought they'd killed me. It took a little while for the facts to get to him straight.

The Coxton wives and other family and friends were all outside their homes milling about anxiously and comparing notes. I'm sure this scene was repeating in camps all over Harlan County.

Finally Dad, Uncle Lawrence, and J. T. Latham returned from Harlan. Each headed to his own home. Mother recalls it like this:

I saw Lawrence before I saw Carl. I was in front of our house and I saw Lawrence in the distance, walking up the road, going home.

Then I saw Carl. I was on the front porch and he was coming up the sidewalk toward the house. Oh God, honey, that's the saddest looking person you've ever seen in your life. He had blood on him and he was carrying a sack. He was carrying Chalk's possessions from the morgue.

Carl was awful for a year or more...an absolute mess. You couldn't mention Chalk without him crying. He couldn't look at one of Chalk's four kids without crying.

He'd go out at night with Floyd Tippet and other buddies, trying to find out who killed Chalk. It made me crazy. I'd say, 'Please Carl, you don't know who did it. You might kill some innocent person!' Really, he never did get over it to his dying day.

In the parcel under Dad's arm was Uncle Chalk's black fedora [the one on the elevator], his bank [mining] clothes consisting of overalls, shirt, and boots, and his personal effects. Included in the latter were Chalk's cigarettes and his union card.[50] Chalk's personal effects should have included a Colt .45, which belonged to his father-in-law, Elihue Bailey. The Colt was missing, however. The assassin, or one of his cohorts, had stolen it off Chalk's dead body. They left the few bullets he had in his pocket, and Dad had them with him.

As best as can be ascertained, here is how Chalk Ruth spent his last day on earth. After the early morning picket at the Kitts mine, the miners broke for breakfast. Some went home, as did Dad and Uncle Lawrence. This was convenient for, as I have said, Kitts and Coxton are close in proximity. Some went on to Harlan to eat there. Dad asked Chalk to come home with him for breakfast, but he had already made plans to eat with the group of miners going to Harlan to eat at Sally Howard's restaurant,[51] on Main Street. In addition to being a first-rate cook, Sally was a real friend to the miners and their cause. Dad says, "Sally's restaurant was on Main Street there, like you was a-goin' to the depot. Them that was with Chalk told me later what a fine breakfast he had eat. Well, I said, I'm shore glad he didn't die hungry."

The miners planned to meet back up after breakfast on 1st Street, at the side of the courthouse in Harlan, near Friday's Radio Shop. From there, they intended to head out for Mary Helen to picket. Dad says:

I'll never forget it. We was standin' there talkin' at the corner of Eversole Street [between 1st and Main], and somebody come up behind me and pulled my hat down over my eyes. I had a gray fedora and Chalk had a black one. Well, I turned around and threw my fists up and there stood Chalk with his up a-laughin'. We all had a good laugh, me and Chalk a-standin' there like we was fixin' to spar and me with my hat down over my eyes. We was just a-jokin' around, you know.

This was the last time Dad and Chalk would ever laugh together. He didn't know it, but this was to be the last time Dad would ever see his dearly-loved brother alive.

The miners loaded up and left Harlan. They drove to Mary Helen and picketed there, as described earlier, and then went to Crummies Creek. Unbeknown to Dad, Chalk was one of those who had gone into the company store with some others to get a "co-cola."

They had went in there to get them a co-cola. Chalk had turned around, they said, like at the meat case or somethin' and was facin' away. And back behind, on the meat block, they had a machine gun or a B.A.R. set up. They had it covered with a butcher's apron.

When the shootin' cut loose from the machine guns outside and up in that gable, Chalk and the other miners turned toward the door and was about to go out. That's when the thug cut loose on 'em with that machine gun. The coward shot 'em all in the back, I reckon. I know Chalk was. The other miners was Virgil Hampton and Ed Tye. [Again, Dad did not know at the time about Oscar

Goodlin, the miner from Lynch, who was also in the store, and also murdered.]

It was a break of fortune that Dad had no knowledge of Chalk's whereabouts. Had he known Chalk had been killed, another Ruth son would have died that day. There is no way, no way, Dad would have left there alive.

Dad asks Mother, "What's that undertaker I liked, honey?"

Mother answers, "Let's see...Oh! Cunningham."

"That's him! Leonard Cunningham." says Dad. He goes on:

He drove the ambulance, honey. When he come to get Chalk and them at the store he heard a racket when he was waitin' for them to open the door. He said you could tell by the sound that they was a-draggin' somethin' across the floor. Them company men that was inside was a-draggin' somethin'.

Leonard shouted through the door that he had come for the bodies and he said that they was delayed about comin' and openin' the door. And he told them, he said, 'Open this damn door or I'll ram this ambulance through it!'

They opened the door and Leonard said you could see a smeared blood trail like they'd drug a butchered hog. They had drug their man or men away, you see. Leonard said he didn't know how many of their men they had drug away and didn't care, for he saw men that he knew a-layin' there dead [the miners], and his attention was on them. The shooting that killed the gun thug or thugs inside had to come from outside for them miners that was inside was just plain ambushed from the back. They didn't have a chance to do no shootin'.

It never did get out about them thugs, I don't reckon. I don't know who they was or how many they was in there. I don't know if any of them was dead. It never did get out, as far as I know. [The story is that some of the assassins were killed and that their bodies were taken by their confederates to a hangout they had on top of Crummies Mountain and burned to avoid disclosure.]

Uncle Chalk was 27 years old when he was shot down. He left a young wife, Rosa, and four children: Charles Jr., age four, Charlene, age three, Bobby, age two, and Janice, age three months. To my remembrance, I have never met any of the children, but they are my first cousins.

Chalk's body lay in state at Cawood Funeral Home. His funeral was held in the Evarts High School gymnasium, because no other facility was large enough for the anticipated crowd. As it turns out, neither was the gym:

I don't know how many of them there was but they was so many they had to put speakers outside for all of them that couldn't get in the gym. They was so many they couldn't get inside and they had to put speakers outside, honey. They say the sidewalks was filled with people a-listenin' to the funeral service. The UMWA took care of all cost, I know that. It did for them other miners that was killed too.

Mother remembers a chilling account from the time Chalk lay in state at the funeral home and at the funeral itself. "The attendants cautioned the family to be very careful and not touch his face. They had to use so very much wax to make his face presentable, it didn't need to be touched. Really, it should have been a closed coffin."

The outpouring of support for the surviving families of the slain miners was a sight to behold, say Mother and Dad. "Their fellow miners and the UMWA saw that they didn't want for a thing," recounts Dad. Tragically, no one could give them back that which they most wanted.

Dad says that from the time of Chalk's death, his parents began to deteriorate. Although Grandma would not die until 1956, Grandpa passed two years later. "They was just never the same after that," recalls Dad. "The grief just got 'em." Given this, it is fitting that Grandpa, Grandma, and Chalk are buried side-by-side in Burkhart cemetery in Evarts. Their bodies lie on the extreme right side of that little cemetery near the rear, just under a copse of trees. Uncle Chalk's tombstone reads:

Charles

Chalk

Ruth

May 20, 1913 – April 2, 1941

Below the dates of his life is an inscription from the 15th chapter of the Gospel of John: "Greater love hath no man than this, that a man lay down his life for his friends."

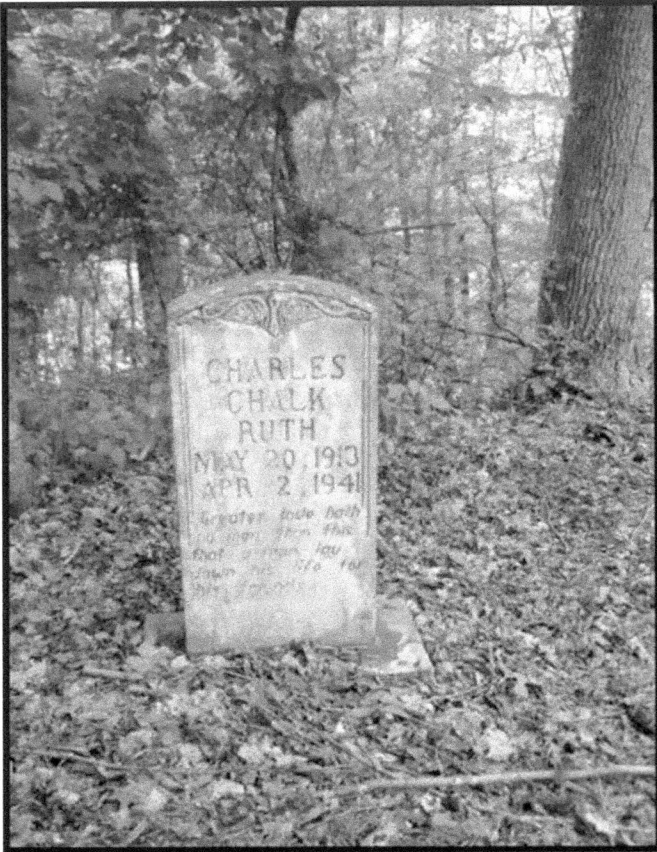

Figure 15. Uncle Chalk's grave

It always strikes me as ironic that the Battle of Evarts has the notoriety, while four times as many miners died in the ambush at Crummies Creek. (One miner died in Evarts, four in Crummies Creek.) There is no doubt whatsoever that what the picketing miners faced at Crummies was a premeditated ambush. The readiness of the machine guns, both in the commissary and in the surrounding mountains, a readiness which had the target triangulated from high ground, proves this. (This type of setup creates what the military calls a "kill box.")

A young girl, Becky Simpson, had gone to Crummies store with her mother that morning, just before the machine guns cut loose. Becky, who was six years old at that time, says the following:

> This big bald-headed guy, they called him Big Jim Black Hair, he was a big-league ballplayer, he told my mother, 'What're you doing here with this child today? Get what little you're going to and get this child back out, there's gon' be trouble today.' As we was leaving the commissary, they was rolling up these big machine guns, that they could open up the double doors and shoot out. So me and Mommy is walking back up the mountain, we heared the shooting start. And they just mowed the men down.[52]

Ben Campagnari, a miner on that fateful picket says:

> Now, we were running, and we had a pegleg man. You wouldn't believe it. Going down that railroad track, and he's hitting about four ties at a time; and he outrun half of the people that had good legs, and we was all a-running because they was cutting us down with the machine gun, or trying to... And I said: 'If I ever go on a picket line again, I'll go with protection.' We died just like ducks.[53]

So I wonder again, why is the ambush at Crummies Creek so little known? (And why in the world did the Kentucky Historical Society or *somebody* not preserve the building that housed the company store?) This tragedy is certainly no less significant than the more famous Battle of Evarts, ten years earlier. Further, I would argue that Crummies Creek is blatantly more diabolical. The Battle of Evarts had two equally armed groups of combatants. Crummies Creek was a dry-gulching.

Perhaps it is because the Battle of Evarts played out on a larger stage, or because its aftermath lasted longer (the actual duration of both "battles" was about the same). Perhaps it is because only miners were verifiably killed in Crummies, while three "deputies" were also killed in Evarts. Perhaps it is because the coal money that hired them used their national contacts and their capital to turn the deputies' deaths at the Battle of Evarts into propaganda in national newspapers. (The *Chicago Tribune's* favorite terms for the union miners seem to have been "mob" and "labor goons."[54]) I do not know the answer to my question. But still I wonder.

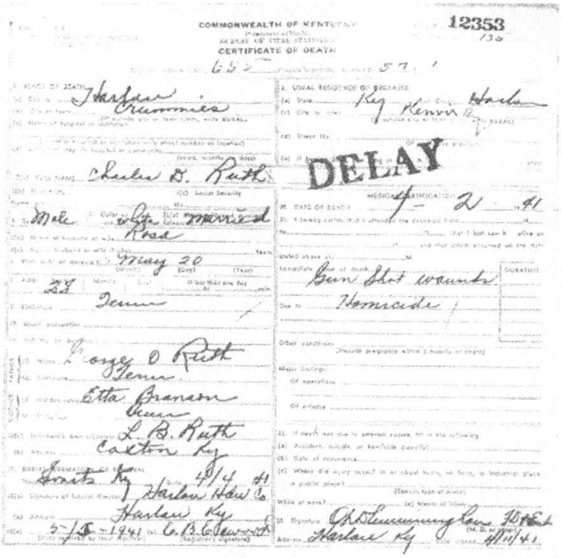
COMMONWEALTH OF KENTUCKY
CERTIFICATE OF DEATH
12353
DELAY
Harlan
Crummies
Charles B. Ruth
Gun Shot wounds
Homicide

Figure 16. Uncle Chalk's death certificate

PART TWO

COXTON TO
BLACK MOUNTAIN

CHAPTER 7

31 Camp

Mother and Dad moved from Coxton to Black Mountain's 31 Camp in the spring of 1942. As Dad was a miner at 31, this move just made sense. The mine was in walking distance from house #1039 (each camp house displayed its number above the front door), where they now lived. Peabody Coal Company charged $10.00 a month for rent on the house. The amount was deducted monthly from the miner's pay. Peabody actually ran a picture of the house in their periodical of the day. They chose Mother and Dad's house because of how well they maintained the house and the yard. (The house exists to this day. It has been renovated and enlarged and is owned and lived in by a close friend of my oldest sister, Pat.)

My sister Pat was just over two years old at the time of the move and the family was about to grow by one more. My maternal grandmother, Laura Vaughn, moved in with Mother and Dad. She lived with our family from then on, until her death in 1993, at the age of 102. We children always considered ourselves doubly blessed to have a great Mother and Mom (for that is what we called her). It was like having two Mothers – two wonderful Mothers.

Mom was a remarkable woman. She was a country healer to whom many a folk came with their ailments and injuries. Herbs and mountain remedies (and snuff!) were her medicines and treatments. She was also a midwife. In that capacity she delivered a number of babies including one of the sons[55] of Mother and Dad's neighbors, Ned and Dora Montgomery. (Ned Montgomery died in a mining accident at 31 in 1955. He was 43.)

Figure 17. Mother and Dad's house in 31 Camp, Black Mountain
(Courtesy National Archives. Used by permission.)

The Black Mountain years were the favorite of all for both Mother and Dad. They remember Camps 30 and 31 to be delightful, fun neighborhoods, full of character and characters! However, some of what awaited them in Black Mountain, Mother found very troubling. She says:

When we first moved there I thought 'Golly, what have we got in to?' It seemed like half the women were stepping out on their husbands and half the husbands were stepping out on their wives. Some of the men, when they were going out with their buddies, used to say they were married until they got to the Evarts bridge. When they got there they would take their wedding ring off. And they said they were married again once they crossed the bridge back into Evarts. They'd put their wedding band back on.

All the houses in 31 Camp were painted in a similar motif – white with green trim – and many residents prided themselves on their lawns and their flowers and their white-washed trees.

Lights came on all around the camp early, as the 4:30 whistle came screaming down the tracks every workday morning from the tipple. Mothers and wives would begin to fix breakfast as their miners prepared for the shift ahead. Women would see their men off at the door or from the front porch, and the tracks would fill with miners heading down to the tipple.

We hear this phrase tossed about now in society and in churches but the term truly applied to Black Mountain in the 1940s. They were a community.[56] People knew one another. They laughed together and cried together. They fought common enemies and even, sometimes, each other. They danced and partied together. They prayed and worshipped together. In short, they pulled together.

Dad certainly did his fair share of that pulling. Mother says, "When people around us needed things done they always called on Carl." Here are two examples, both of which just happen to involve Mother and Dad's neighbors, the Stoners. Mother remembers:

Oliver Stoner's mother [who lived with the Stoners] had to have her right arm removed. I can't recall why. They took it off there at the company hospital in 30. They had the hospital pack the arm up so they could bring it home. See, many people believed that if you lost an arm or a leg or something and it wasn't prepared correctly and then buried properly, it would ache you the rest of your life [phantom pain].

When they got home they called Carl over and asked him if he would bury Mrs. Stoner's arm. You know Carl, he was glad to do it for them. He either got or made, I can't recall which, a box just the right size to put the arm in. He straightened the arm and hand out and put cotton between the fingers to keep them straight and spaced right, and then he wrapped the arm and hand and put it in the box. He took it to the cemetery up there behind #2 Camp [in 31] like you were going to Punkin Center[57] and buried it. Like a lot of the people up there, the Stoners believed this would keep her from having pain from that arm.

The second story has Dad playing the role of a veterinarian. As Dad tells the story:

Oliver [Stoner] had bought a black calf that he kept fenced in behind their house. That calf would figure a way to get the gate open and would get out. It would get in the neighbors' yards and trample the flowers and make a mess. Somebody got tired of that buddy and caught that calf in the side with an ax! Nobody never did know who did it but whoever it was put a big gash in that calf's side. Oliver had the vet sew it up but the stitchin' didn't hold and it busted loose.

Oliver was a-tellin' me about it and I said I'd fix it for him. He said he'd shore appreciate it if I would. I got me an ice pick and smithed it [worked on it like a blacksmith] and turned it into a needle. It looked just like a big needle when I was through with it. I used 25-pound-test fishin' line, that black Japan silk fishin' line I liked for catfishin', for thread. We throwed that calf [brought it to the ground] in our front yard and I had some of 'em tie its front and back legs so it couldn't kick.

Well, I just set astride that calf while some of 'em held its legs so it couldn't buck and such. I got what was left of that vet's thread out of its skin and then I stitched the gash up. It healed up completely before too long. The scar even haired-over, in time.

The vet come through some time after that and looked at the calf and told Oliver it had healed just fine and that the stitching had done the job. Oliver told him, 'Huh, that ain't your stitchin', Doc. Yours come loose!' He said, 'My neighbor done that!' Oliver said the vet said, 'Well, he shore did a good job.'

There were a surprising number of activities to get involved with in the camps. The women had a local women's club and the men likewise. As for the latter, the men's clubs were much more informal and unofficial and usually consisted of groups of buddies banded together around hunting, fishing, and gambling – specifically, poker and craps. [I am speaking here about Dad and the men with whom he was close friends, and their activities. There were undoubtedly men who built their life around their church and church activities, around the Masonic and other lodges, around gardening, and so on. These were not the day-to-day running mates of my father.]

Figure 18. Harlan County miners gambling. (Courtesy National Archives. Used by permission.)

For a while, Dad was a member of an organized group called "The Independent Order of Odd Fellows." The Odd Fellows is a good-works fraternity which originated in England. In our country, it dates back to the early 1800s. The "Odd Fellows" wore blue uniforms and billed caps and would dress formally for certain occasions including funerals, if the deceased were a member of their order.

Mother, the undisputed world champion of finicky eaters says, "I tasted my first and only oyster at an Odd Fellows banquet at the Llewellyn Hotel, in Harlan. Note carefully her words – she "tasted" it. "I didn't swallow it. I pretended to wipe my mouth and spit it into my napkin!"

I mentioned that the more common clubs for Dad and his friends were built around camaraderie – fishing, hunting, and gambling. I would add to that team sports. They loved their football, baseball, and basketball and frequently listened to them on the radio. Dad was a die-hard Tennessee fan and took as well as he gave a lot of good-natured ribbing over the outcome of games with Kentucky.

Mother and Dad share a story with me – a sports story – that spotlights one of their friends, Silas Davis. Silas was one of seven children, all of whom were friends of Mother and Dad. The Davis children [not in birth order] were: Leland, Juanita, Fred [known to all as "Blab" and one of Dad's closest friends], Silas, Lucille, Cecil, and Frank.

Dad and some buddies from Black Mountain catch the bus in Harlan to go to a baseball game in Virginia. The ride home is a late one and soon they all fall asleep on the bus. The bus pulls into the terminal in Harlan and to their dismay, one of their number, Silas Davis, is missing!

Dad inquires with the bus driver as to their absent companion, only to be told, "Well, a guy got off in Cawood. He sounds like your friend." On the car ride back to Black Mountain Dad says, "Boys, I'm worried about Silas. If he don't show up in the mornin' [for work] I'm gonna go huntin' him."

The next morning, no Silas. Dad takes the morning off and goes looking for him. In Cawood, he inquires at houses along the highway that are near the bus stop. At one house a man comes to the door and says, "He knocked on my door real late last night and asked me where he was at. He had no idea. He had been wandering, lost. I set him straight as to where he was and he caught the bus home." Dad returns to Black Mountain and goes back to work. Silas is there. He had not shown up for work on time because he has accidentally slept in, given his late and rather bizarre night.

What had happened is this. Silas and his brother Cecil were both notorious sleepwalkers. Turns out Silas had departed the bus in his sleep! He had no idea where he was, nor how he got there, until he knocked on the door of that Good Samaritan in Cawood!

Permit me to share a couple more short stories about the somnambulant Silas. The first catches my eye for its psychoanalytic value. It seems Silas had a recurring dream in which a coal truck is coming off the mountain with a full load of coal. The truck is out of control and careening unchecked straight for the house. Just at impact, Silas would wake up in a panic – and find himself standing out in the yard! Mother says, "They couldn't keep a window in that bedroom because Silas was always breaking them out going out that window to get away from that coal truck!"

Lastly, if a group of friends had been out dancing, or perhaps the men had been playing poker late, Silas would sometimes stay over with Mother and Dad. Dad's response was always the same: "Buddy, you're more than welcome to stay, but I'll be a-settin' up. I ain't about to go to sleep with you a-beddin' down in the house!" Dad had good reason to be on guard. Later Silas would marry. One night his wife, Blanche, woke up to a fright. Reportedly, Silas was standing over her with a knife in his hand. He was sound asleep!

———————————

1943 came forth in sober fashion for Dad. In late January of that year, Grandpa Ruth had a stroke. Dad recalls:

They come to where I was a-droppin' gons to tell me. I took off to Emma's [his sister] for him and Mom was a-livin' with Sis at Shields. When I got there, I went over to him and said, 'Dad, do you know who this is?' He looked at me with a feeble look. I don't know if he knowed me or not.

I don't know what he died of.[58] I reckon it was somethin' with his heart. His feet and legs was swollen somethin' awful for some time. He couldn't sleep a layin' down and they'd fixed a little bench like over his chair with a pillar [pillow] and he'd fold his arms and lay over on it to sleep. He couldn't breathe if he was a layin' down. He slept that way for nine months, the last nine months of his life.

119

Dad was a big joker and they said he joked right up to the last minute. He loved to make people laugh. I reckon that's where I got that.

The night he died he told 'em at Emma's, 'you kids go on to bed now.' He knowed he was about to die. He didn't want them to have to see it.

Grandpa Ruth was 67 years old at the time of his death.

Dad was a weigh master at the mines at the time. His job was to move the loaded gons to the scales to weigh them, and then move ("drop") them on down the track. His last task on every loaded car of coal was to randomly place a heart-shaped red sticker on the blocks of coal on the top of each carload. The sticker was the logo of the Peabody Coal Company (owner of the Black Mountain Coal Company) and printed on each in silver was their brand name "Great Heart Coal." The powerful diesel locomotives would come in the evening ["of a-evenin'"] and haul the coal away.

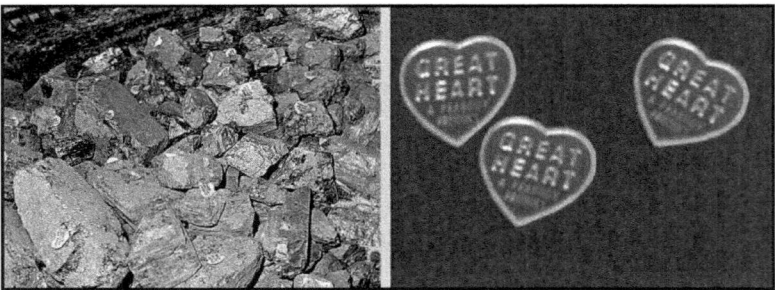

Figure 19. Left: Gon of Black Mountain's finest with "Great Heart Coal" stickers applied. (Courtesy National Archives. Used by permission.) Right: Close-up of the Great Heart Stickers. (Picture taken from exhibit at Kentucky Coal Mining Museum in Benham.)

Mother was like Dad in that her best friend in all the world was one of her siblings. Mother loved her older sister Goldie and, until Aunt Goldie's dying day, did all she could to care for her. But Mother and Dollie, the youngest of the three girls, were inseparable best friends. In fact, Dollie lived with Mother and Dad "a good while" at 31 until she and Sine Smith married.

Figure 20. Left to right, Dollie, Dad, Mother (holding Ronnie), Pat, and Mom. Dollie lived with Mother and Dad at this time, prior to marrying Sine. (Courtesy National Archives. Used by permission.)

Once married, Dollie and Sine lived across the road from Mother and Dad in 31 Camp. Their two sons, Bill and Larry, were born to them during that time. As Mother and Dollie were so often together, it follows that so were their children. My older siblings and Bill and

Larry grew up together as close as brothers and sisters. I was the last to come along and can testify to the same. Bill and Larry are like brothers to me. Later, the Smiths moved to #2 Camp in 30. Sine's father had passed away and they moved to 30 to be closer to his mother.

After seeing to their morning chores women would visit together on front porches over cups of coffee and homemade goodies. (Mother and Dollie and their little ones typically spent their days together until cooking time.) Camp wives enjoyed each other's company and inwardly worried about their men. What they hoped and prayed for on any given day was a certain kind of silence. They hoped they wouldn't hear an irregular mine whistle or the siren of the ambulance. The former meant there had been a major catastrophe at the mine; the latter meant that an accident had occurred, significant enough to call for an ambulance. Although it had not been her first time, nor would it be her last, Mother would hear that sound and see the sight of the ambulance early one morning in February, 1944. Dad says:

> I was working the night shift then, a-doublin' back. This was in the war years, you see, and the company would let you work up to three doubles in one week. I worked the day shift but this was one of them days I was a-doublin' back to make extra money.
>
> I was comin' out by the tram with six sets of batteries. Each battery weighed a thousand pounds. You put them on the side of the shuttle car to run it, you see.
>
> What you'd do is take them batteries down to the motor barn and put them in the battery space

down there and charge 'em up. You'd charge 'em so they'd keep enough juice to do a shift, you see. We'd wait until the shift was over with, til the night shift was done. Then we'd go in there to grease the machinery and change the batteries, you see, and get ready for the day shift.

Well, I had started out of the mine with six sets of batteries and I got out and called on the phone for the road [the right of way, the track]. The traffic man told me to come on down, that I had the right of way.

Another feller was going to move a load of coal to the third left entry to get out of my way, to clear the road. We wasn't a-runnin' that section at the time, you see. It had worked out. We'd use that section to sidetrack loaded cars in the winter time, to keep rain and snow off the coal.

Anyway, he was supposed to have been down there a-blockin' the road for me. So I started down. I was runnin' the motor and I'd look up over the top of the motor watchin' for traffic on the road, just to be sure. Then I thought I seen somethin' like the bulk of a car and I kept lookin' and shore enough, it was. And I thanks, 'Lord have mercy, there sets that trip of coal!'

We had beams across the top and timbers set in there because it was bad top [i.e., an unstable roof]. I knowed if I wrecked and hit one of them beams the whole thing would fall in on us.

I was haulin' out Jim Angel, he had bummed a ride out, and Claude Stanley was with me. He was a-helpin' me change out the batteries. Jim was ridin' on the front of the car, I believe, right behind the motor, and Claude was ridin' on the back end of the last car, I think. I'm in the motor, runnin' it. [Mother thinks Claude Stanley got out of mining later on, and opened a barbershop in Evarts.]

When I seen that trip of coal a-settin' there I shut her off, but them heavy batteries we was takin' out was a-pushin' us down the hill. I was spinnin' that brake wheel with all I had buddy, but there was just too much weight a-shovin' us on down.

The other feller [parking the coal] had started movin' again and that's one thing that kept us from hittin' him hard. He was a-gatherin' slack in his cars and gettin' 'em to the other section and he had 'em on the move.

When I seen what was happenin' I hollered for Jim and Claude to jump. And see, I was sittin' down here in the deck, over here in the deck of the motor [he illustrates]. See, it's in the center of the motor kindly [kind of]. Well, the headlight was over hear you see, and the controllers. I had to make a hook dive like, to get over and around all that.

I knowed if I clipped them timbers and that bad top come down on us, we'd be goners shore enough. Them two jumped out and I had my hand out, like I was a-divin', to check my fall when I jumped. And I cleared everywhere but my left hip, here.

I dove out the left side of the motor and that front battery car – they had an arm up like this [he illustrates] and a brace to brace them on each side. That arm struck me in the hip and when it did, it throwed me around workways with the track. The outside of my left hand hit the rail and kindly straddled it. The wheel run over my hand. From just about right here on [illustrates by designating on his left hand] it wasn't hurt. From here back it just caught it and ground it up. It hit me so hard that it ripped my little finger loose from my hand. It looked like guts down in there. There was blood and ground meat and rock and shale all mixed.

The wheel didn't cut my finger plumb off. It just ripped it loose from my hand and ground it flat. It busted it all to pieces. I'll never forget, the very tip end of my little finger wasn't even hurt. That finger was layin' back against my wrist. The wreck had ripped up my glove and I finally managed to get it off. All that was holdin' the little finger and the left side of my hand on was a little piece of skin.

Our motor car had hit the other feller's load in the rear, but it didn't wreck, didn't jump the track or nothin'. We'd slowed down just enough and he had commenced a-movin' forward and I guess all that was just enough to keep us from jumpin' the track and hittin' them timbers.

Jim and them was so shook up from it all, and especially after seeing my hand, that they couldn't call for the road out. I said, 'Fellers, I messed up. I'm shore glad you're alright. Can one of y'all pull the motor on out of here to the mouth [of the mine], and call for the road again?'

They was so shook up they couldn't. I got in the motor and run it out the mouth. I had to get out and call for the road. They was so shook they couldn't do it, buddy. I told 'em down there to get somebody else to change the batteries, so that wouldn't be messed up for the next shift, and drove on out of there. I told 'em I could walk around to the head house [where the coal begins its journey via conveyor belt down to the tipple]. It was just about a mile.

They said, 'No! No! You stay there!' They'd called the ambulance, you see. Buddy Smith, Sine's brother, drove the ambulance for the mine. [Bud Smith was also a pilot, who owned his own plane. He was known as "The Flying Miner of Kenvir."]

Somebody up at the mine told Dad to get in the track car so he could take him off the hill. Never one to miss the chance for a good line, Dad replied, "Buddy, they ain't nothin' wrong with my legs. One of my knees is skinned a little bit where I made contact, but I can walk off the hill!" The man just chuckled and shook his head and said, "Lord have mercy, Carl!"

When I got down, Buddy Smith was there a-waitin' on me. I said, 'Bud, take me by the house first.' I always told Della that if anything bad happened I'd let her know it first if I could. I went in the house with my hand behind me. They bandaged it up kindly [kind of] at the motor barn, as best they could.

Della started to reach around me and grab at my hand. I pushed her back. I shore didn't want her to grab that hand! [Mother interjects: 'I tell you, I just about passed out.'] I tell you Mike, it was the funniest thing. From that joint back [from last knuckle of little finger to tip of finger] it wasn't hurt a bit. My fingernail wasn't even bothered. But the rest of that finger and the side of my hand was just gone, buddy.

Bud was about to take me to the hospital. It was there on 30 hill. Bless her heart, I remember Della kept saying, 'Carl, tell them to try and save your hand.' All she could see was that bloody bandage and man was it bloody! She didn't know what my hand looked like.

We got to the hospital and I saw Doc Ruley. If it hadn't been for him I think they'd a-took my hand off. He said to me, 'Carl, you ain't got much left, but I'll do the best I can.' He told me right off they was no savin' that little finger, but I knowed that. It was gone, buddy!

Doc Ruley was somethin' else. He done a great job to save this finger [ring finger]. If you'd a seen it you'd a thought he'd have to take that one too. The space between my little finger and this one was cut plumb through. He took off my little finger and all that stuff that was crushed and used that skin somehow to remake the left side of my hand. For some time after it looked like I might lose all them other fingers too. They was blue-black for a good while.

When the feelin' started comin' back in that thing after Doc Ruley was done, man that hurt! See, that's where your feelin' sensations are – in your fingers. He said to me, 'Carl, it wouldn't have hurt you as bad if you'd had your arm cut off.'[59]

Mother had planned a birthday party for my sister Pat's fourth birthday, still the only child at the time, which was to take place in two days. She was going to call it off in light of Dad's accident. He wouldn't hear of it. "There ain't no need, honey. Doc Ruley will have me so doped up I won't know what's goin' on anyway." Dad was 27 years old and mining had now cost him most of his left thumb and the left side of that same hand, including his little finger.

_____

Practical jokes were an everyday occurrence among the miners. This was a give-and-take ritual among them and a kind of rite of passage. The miner who couldn't take a joke had no chance of making it to the inner circle of the fellowship. Several of my favorite stories growing out of this camaraderie follow. Though I heard these repeated many times over the years, I never tired of hearing Dad tell them, or lost my enjoyment over how he told them.

A friend of ours, Hubert Poore, was in the service [WWII] and was home on leave. His leave was up and he had to return to California and ship back out. He said, 'Carl, when I get back to California, I'll send you a crate of oranges.'

I said, 'Well thank you, buddy. I appreciate that!' That was awful nice of him but I was a-thinkin' to myself, 'What in the world am I goin' to do with a whole crate of oranges?'

Oliver Stoner, our next door neighbor said, 'Carl, I'll buy half of 'em off you.' I said, 'Why no, buddy. I ain't gonna charge you for 'em, for they're give to me.' Oliver said, 'I tell you what then, I'll pay half of the C.O.D. when they get here.' I said that'd be okay.

Oliver's brother, I believe that his name was Houston, lived with Oliver and them. Houston was nearly blind, I remember. He went to the post office [Kenvir] to get their mail and when he come back, he come over to the house and told me that

John [the postmaster, John Vandervelt] said my oranges was in.

Buddy, I headed off to the post office to get them oranges. Oliver and Houston went with me. When I walked up to the window, John said, 'Just a minute Carl, I'll get them.'

He come back with a little 3 x 4 inch crate full of plastic oranges about the size of marbles. We laughed our heads off! Houston and John was in on it, you see. Me and Oliver was caught blind, buddy!

There was a note attached to the crate from Hubert. It said, 'Here are the oranges I promised you Carl. Hope you enjoy them!'

Here's another:

They was a wreck on the track headin' into the mines. I believe the man trip[60] had wrecked. Well, we knocked off work because it was gonna take the rest of the shift to clean up the wreck. Me and Elmer Martin decided we'd just go huntin'. We got up in them mountains and dreckly [directly] I seen this big ol' timber rattler. Man, it was a big'n! It had thirteen rattles and a button! I caught that rattler and said to Elmer, 'I'm gonna have some fun with this.' We went back down the mountain.

I was lookin' for K. P. Floyd. He was a boss at the mine. K. P. was a good guy, a real good guy. [Mother adds, 'He was such a fine man, and a good boss. Everybody liked him. I never heard anybody say a bad word about K. P.'] He was scared to death of snakes, any snake. He was even scared of black snakes! Well, I found him in the bosses' bathroom. I had that rattler behind my back and pulled it out and said, 'Boy, ain't this a pretty'n, K. P.!'

K. P.'s eyes got big as saucers! He backed plumb up in the corner and said, 'I'll hurt you, Carl! I'll hurt you!' All of us in there was a-laughin' up a storm! K. P. was buck naked; he had just took his shower and all he had was a towel. But he just kept sayin', 'I'll hurt you, Carl. I'll hurt you!' They wasn't no way I was gonna put it on him or anything, of course. I knowed how scared he was of snakes and I wouldn't have done that for nothin' in this world. K. P. knowed I wouldn't, of course, but he was still scared of that rattler! We was just havin' a good time.

I took it outside then and showed it to Vardie [McPeek] and them. I killed it and kept its rattlers.

K. P. Floyd, by the way, was first cousin to Charles Arthur Floyd, more commonly known as "Pretty Boy" Floyd.

Figure 21. Miners exiting man trip at end of shift. (Courtesy Dave Johnson. Used by permission.)

One of my favorite stories occurred on the return from
a rabbit hunting trip across the line into Tennessee.
Dad wasn't aboard this time, but recounts the story:

Vardie McPeek was one of the mine
superintendents. We called him Kingfish, because
he was a high up. Frank White was there; he was
a foreman. Homer Mulkey and another miner or
two was with 'em. They was on the way back to
Black Mountain from rabbit huntin'. As they got
to 33 Bridge Vardie shouted, 'Stop this car! Stop
right here; just pull off!'

Vardie, lookin' dead serious said, 'They ain't a
one of you in the crowd that's got any bone in
your nose [manly courage] if you don't foller me!'

Vardie jumped out of that car, and it was a-
gettin' about dusky-dark. He took off down the
bank there, in under 33 Bridge, where you go
down this end of the bridge, on the Tennessee
side. He went under there and he seen an old
snag of a stump a-layin' there on the bank under
the bridge and he took it and slung it out in the
lake. Well, shortly here come Homer, Homer
Mulkey, right behind him, buddy.

Well, Vardie had humped back up there by the
abutment of the bridge, you see. He was in the
dark and Homer and them couldn't see him.

Homer, a-thinkin' Vardie had dove in the water,
come runnin' down through there, buddy, and he
didn't stop, pause, or nothin'. He just hit that
lake, he busted it wide open, buddy!

Vardie was hunkered up there on the bank a-
laughin' at him! He stepped out of the dark and
he was belly laughin' buddy. He was dry as a

bone! The others was there by then and did they take to laughin'!

Homer swam over to the bank and said to Vardie, 'Well, help me out, buddy!'

Vardie said, 'Huh-uh, noooo. They ain't no way that's gonna happen!'

He knowed, you see, Homer was plannin' to pull him in, shore as the world!

They all told it at work the next day and we all got such a kick outta that. That's one thing, you see, we'd always tell, share our stories with each other like that! We'd tell 'em on ourselves just as well as on the next feller.

Finally:

Jim Middleton and some of our fishin' buddies was down on Cherokee Lake [Tennessee], fishin'. Well, they was down there and a storm was comin' up. Cherokee's a big lake and buddy, it gets rough when the wind gets up. I've been on it when the weather would get bad and the white caps would take your boat as high as this ceilin'.

Well, they pulled into the bank a-gettin' off that lake before the storm hit and left the boat. They walked through the woods to the car and got their stuff and carried it down to the bank. They was a-makin' camp, you see. They was a-comin' around the point where they had banked the boat.

They told Jim, while they set up camp, to go get the boat. They wanted him to walk around the point to the boat and drive it back to the campsite. They wanted to get the boat up in the cove there, out of the wind and rain. They said they'd set up camp and get to cookin' their supper while he did that.

Well, they said all of a sudden they heard the awfulest racket a-goin' on and they seen the bushes a shakin' and everything and wondered what in the world was a-goin' on.

One of 'em went to look and see and he said here come Jim with a chain throwed across his shoulder a-pullin' that boat, draggin' it across the knoll!

They was a-bustin' out laughin', buddy! They said, 'Jim, what in the world are you doin'! We meant for you to drive it around the point in here to the cove!' Jim said, 'You'ns didn't say nothin' about drivin' it around. You'ns[61] just told me to go get the boat!'

He had taken across the knob with that chain throwed across his back, buddy, and was a-draggin' boat, motor, and all through the woods to the camp!

In the summer of 1946, Mother gave birth to their second child, Ronnie. Like Pat before him and Sandra after him, Ronnie was born at home. Mother says, "He could have been born at the hospital. Well, Pat could have too, as far as that goes, but I was so backwards then I didn't want to do that. Back then, the doctor would come to your house if you wanted to have the baby at home." Ronnie was, and always would be, the apple of Dad's eye. He is a fine, fine man – a "good Christian man," as Dad said of his own brothers, Lawrence and Ed.

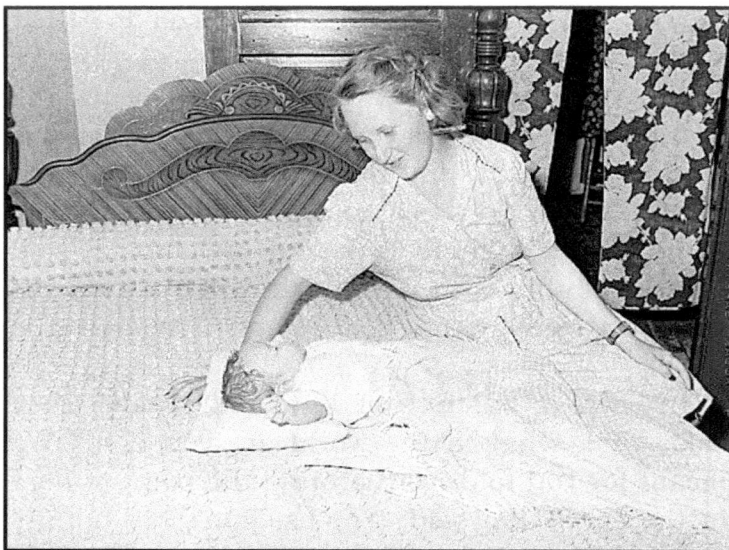

Figure 22. Mother with the infant Ronnie at home in Black Mountain.
(Courtesy of National Archives. Used by permission.)

Being 1946, VE Day and VJ Day were now past. The war was over. With the end of the war came a surcease in the war's rabid demand for coal. While peacetime America still had a high need for the bituminous rock, the life of the mines returned to a more normal schedule. For many of the miners, more free time meant more hunting and fishing.

Dad was a mountain goat. He could climb those hills like he was born to it. It was said that when it came to trudging, he and Arthur Barnes were in a league of their own. Both Mother and Dad liked Mr. Barnes (and his wife, Merthel) a lot. Mother states, "He was a good friend of Carl's. Outside of Sine [Smith], Carl thought Arthur Barnes was the best man alive." She adds, "He was a good guy, a wonderful guy." Mr. Barnes didn't drink alcohol, but when the guys would be hunting or fishing, he would chip in and help pay for their beer, according to Mother.

It would be hard to say which Dad liked best – being in a mine, on a mountain, or on a lake. These were undoubtedly his favorite places on God's good earth. One thing for certain, he absolutely loved to be up in the woods. "I could sit under a tree all day and watch a squirrel cut on a hickory nut," I've heard him say many times. Dad was always more at home in the world of nature than the world of man.

Dad loved to rabbit and squirrel hunt. He loved to gig frogs. You gig frogs at night, so some manner of illumination is required. Instead of the standard headlamp, Dad used his miner's light, his carbide light,[62] when he went gigging. (Miner lights have evolved over the eras from a candle mounted on the front of a cap, to a diminutive lamp with a wick fueled by kerosene or coal oil, to a carbide light, to today's battery-powered model. A carbide light produces the gas acetylene, which it then uses as its energy source. The gas is made by mixing calcium carbide with water inside the unit's reservoir. Dad gave me his carbide light years ago. It is prominently displayed in my office.)

I asked Mother if she prepared and cooked the fish and game Dad came in with. "Shooo no!" she replied. "He'd have to cut up the rabbits and squirrels and frogs and clean the fish. Then he'd have to fry it – if he got it! I wasn't about to fool with that stuff!"

––––––––––––––––––

Mother was an unusual member of their group of friends because she didn't drink (neither did her mom, nor her sisters Goldie or Dollie). In fact, she has never had a drop of alcohol in her life. Mother was a designated driver long before the term came to prominence.

As far as couples' activities were concerned, dancing topped the bill. Some of Mother and Dad's best times in the mining years are associated with nights out dancing with their friends. One of their favorite local spots was just above Evarts towards Shields. There was a little restaurant there owned by Joe Lester. Mother states, "They had a few booths, a jukebox, and a small dance floor." (Although Mother did not, most adults smoked in those days. For fun, Dad would take his carbide light along, strike it and set it on their table so everyone would have a handy light for their cigarettes.)

Figure 23. Dad's carbide light and anemometer (wind gauge)

Mother and Dollie loved to dance...my, how they loved to dance! It was the day of big band, swing, and velvet-throated crooners, soon to be joined by the rock and rollers. It was Glenn Miller and *Moonlight Cocktail* and *In the Mood*, Dick Haynes and *You'll Never Know* ("I've danced that so many times," says Mother). It was Les Brown and Doris Day and *Sentimental Journey*. It was Fats Domino and *Ain't That a Shame* and *Walking to New Orleans*, Duke Ellington's saxophone-rich *Things Ain't What They Used to Be*, Jimmy Forrest and *Night Train*, and Lionel Hampton's *Hamp's Boogie Woogie*. It was *Let the Good Times Roll* and *Tuxedo Junction* and *Pennsylvania 6-5000* and *Chattanooga Choo Choo* and *Shake Rattle and Roll* and *Stagger Lee* and *Whole Lotta Shakin' Goin' On* and *Rock Around the Clock*. It was Carl Perkins and *Blue Suede Shoes* and Elvis and *Hound Dog* and Mother and Dollie loved them all!

Dad and Sine could hang in there slow dancing but when it came to jitterbugging,[63] both Mother and Dollie liked a faster and more skilled pair of feet than either of their husbands possessed. Actually, their favorite jitterbugging partner was each other. They had grown up dancing that still-popular dance together.

On numerous occasions, after an evening of good music and dancing, someone new to the group would approach Dad the next day and say, "Boy, Della was feeling good last night, wasn't she?" [Meaning, from the effect of alcohol.] Dad would laugh and say, "Buddy, she don't drink. She's never had a drop in her life. That's just how much she loves to dance!"

One dancing story I loved to hear happened at "Nigger Head" (named for an adjacent mountain's natural rock outcropping), a popular dance club in Pennington Gap, Virginia. Mother starts this one:

Arthur McFarland was with us and a good jitterbug song came on – it was *In the Mood*, and man, the band was playing it fast - and Arthur came over and asked Dollie to dance. We were all just a big group of friends and we all danced with each other's husbands and the single men in the group. We were all such good friends.

When that jitterbug came on Arthur came over to our table and asked Dollie to dance. The music was real good and Arthur just kind of went wild, or something.

Dad is laughing as Mother is telling this story. You can see in his expression the recall of this memory. Dad jumps in, and picks up the story, still laughing:

I never seen anything like it! We'd brag on him to keep him goin' – to egg him on! Buddy, he was a-runnin' all over that buildin' with poor ol' Dollie! [Mother interjects, 'He wasn't dancing at all, he was just sort of running from corner to corner with Dollie!'] He'd be over there, buddy, and he'd just rare back and here they'd come! He'd come right at you lookin' right wild-eyed. He looked like he had a spell on or somethin'! [Dad is really laughing now!]

Dollie come back to the table when the song was over just a-heavin'. She said, 'Lord have mercy, what came over him? That wore me out!'

Well, another good song come on and I said to Arthur, 'That's a good'n buddy. You better get that'n!' Little ol' Dollie cut her eyes at me. She was scared to death he'd ask her again!

A couple of the guys called me outside. They was a-laughin' their heads off! They said, 'Carl, you reckon you can get him to do that again?' I said, 'I don't know. I'll try.' We went back in and I'd say, 'Arthur, you're gonna miss that song!' And he'd say, 'I can't Carl. I have to wait til the spirit hits me. I just ain't feelin' it yet!'

To Dollie's relief, Mr. McFarland didn't get hit by the spirit or any other force, metaphysical or otherwise, the rest of that evening. That one experience was enough for her, and neither she, nor Mother, nor Dad ever forgot it!

(If I may insert a personal note. Growing up, I remember our home often being filled with good music and dancing. I wouldn't take anything for those memories.)

_____

On the trips I've made to Harlan County, it's hard to imagine it as it was in the '40s. Black Mountain is always described by Mother as a bustling community, alive with activity. As noted, the post office for both 30 and 31 was in Kenvir. Along with a massive company store, Kenvir also had a theater, a restaurant, a drug store/confectionary, a doctor's office, a police station (sans jail), a pool room, and the Black Mountain Hospital, among other businesses. Most of these were, of course, owned by the mining monopoly.

Busses ran the twelve or so miles from Black Mountain to Harlan every thirty minutes during the war years. This fact is staggering to me. To imagine the area as once so active, so thriving that busses ran to that kind of daily schedule amazes me.

Families didn't spend their time secluded to themselves as the majority of us seem to do today. They walked to the company store and elsewhere, and the one mile between 30 and 31 Camps. They visited with one another. They would sit on their porches in the evening and call out to each other from road or track to porch, and stop for a chat. As I said before, everyone knew everyone, and the camps were true communities.

This is not to say, of course, that they were idyllic. Camps 30 and 31 were, after all, populated by humans. There were fallouts and fights and betrayals and stabbings and shootings and, yes, even killings. Harlan County got its moniker "Bloody Harlan" long before mine feuds. The homicide rate in Harlan County in the 1920s was the highest in the nation. Kentucky humorist Irvin Cobb, when explaining why the state's official symbol has two men facing each other and clasping hands quipped, "The intent of the picture is plain. So long as they both hold hands, neither can reach for his hardware."[64] Mother, who lived in downtown Evarts as a child, remembers:

> There'd be a killing in downtown Evarts about every Saturday night. Honest to God, just about every Saturday night somebody was either shot or stabbed, but there would be a killing. I remember one Saturday, we were just kids, Poppa had sent Goldie downtown for something. Dillard Middleton stopped her on the street there and said 'Goldie' – everybody knew everybody, you see – he said, 'Goldie, you need to get off the street and get home, honey. There's gonna be trouble here soon.' Sure enough, somebody got killed. Dillard was just looking out for Goldie and didn't want her to be there when it happened, where she might get hurt somehow.

I can't speak for the present, but the Harlan County mindset of the old days was very much similar to that found throughout Southern Appalachia. It was grounded in the spirit of the Scot and Irish settlers of this part of our country. A sense of family unity was there, anchored in and born out of the clan ethic and ethos common to Scotland and Ireland. (To illustrate, on one trip to Harlan County with Mother, I stopped in Brittians Creek to ask a man working in his yard if he knew the location of a particular neighborhood. His answer, "I don't know where that is. I'm new here. I've only been here sixteen years; I ain't been here that long." Sixteen years and yet he was "new here," and hadn't "been here that long!") Brothers, for example, might fight hammer and tongs with one another but woe to the interloper who did harm! He could expect to soon be facing a swift and certain reckoning. Ever heard of Kentucky/West Virginia's own Hatfield-McCoy feud? Same people, same mindset. (Even in the frontier times the region we now know as Kentucky had a reputation for the warlike nature of its settlers. The native Indians gave the region inhabited by the white settlers a name that translates "dark and bloody ground."[65])

Dad was four-square of this nature and attitude. This is why until his very latest years, Dad wished he had found the man who murdered Chalk. To his bones Dad felt that man had a reckoning coming. In fact, not long after Chalk's death, Dad's brothers Lawrence and Ed tried to calm Dad of his desire and intent for vengeance. Both these brothers were fine Christian men and their message to Dad was, "Carl, you've got to forgive." He was having none of it. Though Dad himself was a Christian, he did not see Chalk's death as these brothers did. He had neither desire nor intent to turn a cheek toward that assassin.

Dad was a conundrum, really. I don't think I've ever seen anyone with a more dichotomous personality. In those mining decades of his life, Dad seemed to be equally one-half Good Samaritan and one-half Billy Hell, with very little neutral zone in the middle. Happily, this would change in Dad's latter years.

I always thought of Dad as an Old Testament character. He wouldn't bother anyone, or harry them in any way. He was as good a neighbor or friend as you could have. But if provoked, Dad didn't have a lot of back up in him and by not a lot, I mean none. He wasn't much of a cheek turner. "Eye for an eye" resonated more with him. Again, this was and, generally speaking, very much still is the native Appalachian mindset.

Dad would do anything for a person, be they close friend or perfect stranger. In fact, I could fill this book with accounts of Dad's acts of benevolence. Literally. I have intentionally left most of these out so as not to give an imbalanced account. For example, if Dad knew of someone who had lost a loved one, or came upon a scene where a complete stranger was digging a loved-one's grave (a common practice in the day), he would stop and do the digging for them. It wouldn't matter if he was in his Sunday best or dressed for work. "I just couldn't stand the thought of somebody a-havin' to dig the grave for their own people. That's just too hard and ought not be." That was Dad. Mother says, "From the tipple he could see if someone was up at the 31 cemetery digging a grave. If he saw that, he would take off work and go dig it for them. He just couldn't stand seeing people having to dig a loved-one's grave."

But he was not to be messed with. Basically, I believe Dad's subterranean fury was anchored to three sources: his natural temperament, his childhood experience of being the youngest boy in the family, and from the stern discipline he and his brothers received from their father. Psychologically, it is an example of the classic nature-nurture dynamic.[66] I would also have to add a fourth factor, one which came into play during adulthood. I am speaking of the heart-breaking injustices and cruelties he saw the miners suffer during those turbulent decades.

Black and white miners worked side-by-side and played side-by-side (though their housing was segregated). I always thought of this as fitting because, although they may have gone into the mine different colors, by the time the shift was over they were all black. These friends played a lot of poker and shot a lot of craps in "Colored Camp." (Colored Camp lay along the road between 30 and 31.) One night, there is a poker game at one of the black miner's homes. Another of those incidents occur which simultaneously shows the intensity of Dad's nature, and makes one wonder what kept him alive.

We was all playin' cards at Nigger John's [this was the name he was known by to one and all, black and white alike] and I caught him a-cheatin'. I slapped him up the side of the head. I was about to start in on him and he jumped up and grabbed his shotgun. I turned and walked out the door to go to my car, my old Ford. I usually had my shotgun in the trunk, but it wasn't there. I told Blab [Davis] to take my car and go get my shotgun. [Even in the midst of so intense a situation, the humorous occurs. When Blab returns, while getting the shotgun out of the trunk, he accidentally trips the trigger – and blows a hole out of the rear quarter panel of Dad's car!] Nigger John come to his porch with his shotgun and took a shot at me, but missed. [Intentionally, I suspect. Unless one is firing a "punkin' ball" or slug, it is *very* hard to miss at close range with a shotgun!]

That made me mad! I started walkin' toward the porch and he was standin' there with his shotgun. I got to fumblin' for my hawkbill [knife – let's just say, a hawkbill isn't designed for whittling] in the bib pocket of my overalls. I got mad, you see, 'cause I couldn't get a-hold of it. I could feel it but I couldn't get a-hold of it. I was a-headin' to his porch and I thanks, 'Well, he'll shoot me once but I'll cut his throat!' I was about up to him when he throwed his shotgun down on the porch and run through his house and out the back door. I picked up a big rock by his porch and throwed it through his front window. It hit midway of it and tore the whole thing out of the wall, frame and all, and just shattered ever bit of glass in it.

Jack McPeek [Vardy's son] was the town law and he come up. He told me not to worry about this, for he had been a-cheatin' at cards. The other colored miners who were in the game, and the other colored miners that had come up there from in the camp because of the ruckus said, 'It's a wonder somebody didn't kill him. He was a-cheatin' at poker!' They wasn't mad at me at all. Color didn't matter; we all knowed each other. They was on my side 'cause he was a-cheatin'.

The funny thing is, "Nigger John" and Dad were the best of friends. This is just the kind of thing that could escalate that quickly in the Black Mountain of the day. This is especially true when there was an offense against the code – like cheating at poker – and when alcohol was involved, as it usually was in such settings.

In fact, John didn't run because he was a coward. Far from it. He ran because he didn't want to kill his good friend, Carl Ruth. He knew Dad would keep advancing. He knew how he was. He didn't want to have to shoot him.

The next day, after tempers subsided and alcohol was out of the system, Dad felt awful about what had happened, and the damage done to John's house. He went that very day, repaired the house, and apologized to his friend. After the previous anomalous night, the two friends would play poker together again – soon and frequently.

John and his wife Lilly would move to Verda (between Harlan and Evarts) sometime later and their home would continue to be the sight of poker games. Mother adds, "Everybody I knew liked John and Lilly. They were good people."

Here is an anecdote about his friend John that Dad liked to tell:

> He's the only guy I ever knowed that actually liked the taste of whiskey. We all drunk it but John *liked* it! He carried his whiskey in a tiny medicine bottle. From time to time he would take the cap off that bottle and lick the mouth of the bottle. He liked the taste of whiskey that much. He liked to wet his lips with it and taste it on his lips.

As we are around the table talking, Mother proffers another gambling story, a brief one, that I do not recall having heard before:

> There was a black miner that everybody called 'Boots.' I don't know what his real name was, I

just know that everybody called him Boots. I remember he had a brother named Maynard. Boots was a real nice man and the finest dresser you've ever seen.

I was at home one night and somebody knocked at the door. It was Boots. Well, Boots handed me $300.00 and said, 'Carl won this in our poker game that's going on down at the camp [Colored Camp]. I wanted to bring it to you before he loaned it out or lost it back.'

Mother was always appreciative of Boots for doing this. He left the game temporarily just to walk that half-mile up to the house and give her this money. It was a very kind gesture. Of a practical note, in a mining camp in the 1940s, $300.00 was a tidy chunk of change!

Figure 24. Houses in "Colored Camp," which lay between 30 and 31. (Courtesy of National Archives. Used by permission.)

Among Dad's best friends in Black Mountain were the afore-mentioned Davis brothers, (especially Blab, Silas, and Cecil), Veck Singo, Roy McKamey, and Junior McPeek [another of Vardy's sons]. Mother adds, "He had a lot of friends. Arthur Barnes and Arthur McFarland [the dancer] were his favorite hunting buddies." The Martin brothers, Elmer and Kelly, were close to Dad, as were Pat Ewell (a sophisticate and lover of opera) and Johnny Wallace. Mother says:

> Johnny Wallace was the one who always made our spaghetti. He was I-tallian [that's how the locals pronounced it, with a long "I"]. Everybody would all show up at our house and Johnny would cook spaghetti.
>
> Also, there was a little restaurant with a small dance floor and a jukebox just above Evarts, like you were going to Shields. We'd all stay after closing time and the couple that owned it – Joe and Elsie Lester – would let Johnny cook spaghetti. We'd eat and dance and have us a time.
>
> I remember one funny thing about that. Some of the gang got to complaining that Johnny put too much red pepper flakes in the sauce. Johnny turned and said, 'If you don't quit complaining, I'll let you make it yourself!'
>
> In just a minute Pat Ewell absent-mindedly slipped and said, 'Man, this spaghetti's hot!' Everybody, including Johnny, turned and looked at him. Thinking on his feet, Pat said, 'And that's just the way I like it!' We all got a good laugh out of that!

Dad and Mother tell a touching story involving Pat Ewell that will occur some twenty years from these days in Black Mountain, when our family lived in Harlan. Mr.

Ewell, in the old days, was a surveyor for the mine. When Black Mountain shut down, he retired to Florida. One summer, about 1963, he took the Greyhound from Florida to Harlan, to visit with old friends. (I actually have a vague memory of meeting Mr. Ewell on that visit.)

Mother, Dad, and their friend visited from early day until evening, revisiting and reliving the old days and good times. At day's end, Mr. Ewell called a taxi and returned downtown to the Llewellyn Hotel, in Harlan. About thirty minutes later, there was a knock at the door. It was Mr. Ewell. He said he enjoyed their visit so much that he just couldn't leave. The three old friends sat around the table with cups of coffee and continued well into the night where they left off. I am glad they had this evening. This was the last time Mother and Dad saw Pat Ewell, who was at that time carrying the cancer that would claim his life later, back in Florida. The last contact they had with him was in the form of a letter from him which included a picture of a trophy fish he caught while deep-sea fishing.

One activity that Mother and Dollie enjoyed was taking in a good movie at the Margie Grand Theater. The Margie Grand (no longer there, though the building remains) was located on the corner of 2nd and Central in Harlan. Although Harlan had another theater, the New Harlan Theater (on South Main Street), Mother and Dollie preferred the Margie Grand (built by and named for Margie Noe). One winter, on a cold December day, the sisters decided to go to the movie. As was their custom, they caught the bus in Coxton and took the three-and-a-half-mile ride into town. It was a lazy

Sunday afternoon, and they were wanting to enjoy themselves.

After the movie, they stepped out of the theater to a frantic Harlan. The area around the courthouse (just across from the Margie Grand) was a boisterous hive of emotional conversation and anxious activity. The date is December, 7, 1941. The Japanese have just attacked Pearl Harbor.

Coal-yard Facts

Coal is mined in 25 states, resulting in more than 800,000 U. S. jobs.

CHAPTER 8

The War Years

The onset of WWII would have a major impact on the Appalachian coal business. A war runs on industry and, as said earlier, industry runs on coal.[67]

Many miners, Dad among them, frequently worked double shifts for the duration of the war. Coal was needed urgently and abundantly. All local miners had jobs, and still more miners were needed. Immigrants came to Harlan County[68] from the Northeast and elsewhere because work was readily available.

One of the ironies of war, if you're on the winning side, is that it is good for the economy. This is true locally as well as nationally, and was certainly true in Black Mountain. "That place was booming," says Mother.

What this did not mean was an infusion of new industries into the area. The coal companies would not allow that. They were not about to relinquish their monopolistic stranglehold (a fact for which the economy of the region is paying to this very day). The coal company owned the store (hence "company" store), and other businesses in and around the camp areas. It was a way of multiplying their profits.

Figure 25. The expansive company store at Lynch (Courtesy National Archives. Used by permission.)

To realize the power in the monopolies, one has only to recognize the fact that they minted their own currency! (Incredulously, this was a common practice that continued into the 1950s until the U. S. Supreme Court stopped it, ruling the use of scrip to be unconstitutional.[69]) Though most mines paid in cash, cash advances were typically given in the form of scrip (tokens), and each mining company minted its own. (A hobby of mine is collecting Harlan County coal scrip.) This, of course, makes the expression "cash advance" a complete misnomer. Scrip wasn't cash.

Figure 26. Scrip from author's private collection. Left to right from top are: a rare piece from Black Mountain Coal Co (pre-Peabody), Black Mountain (Peabody Coal Company), Crummies Creek (2), Belva (Straight Creek Coal), Three Point, Kildav (King Harlan), Lejunior (Cook and Sharpe), and Kitts (Clover Fork Coal Co). Various denominations are shown.

Mother says:

Well, say you needed some money between paydays [Black Mountain paid on the 15th and 30th of the month]. You would take your scrip card with you up to the window and tell them how much you wanted, as long as the miner had pay coming. You could get one dollar, two, five, ten, twenty, whatever you wanted as long as the miner had that much pay coming to him. They would take your scrip card, put their copy with it [one was white, the other pink or yellow, as Mother recalls], and then type or punch out how much you got on that day. Come payday, that amount was withheld from the miner's pay.

This "currency" was useless outside company-owned businesses for the most part. Useless, that is, unless one was willing to take less than face value for the stuff. Peabody scrip from the Black Mountain Coal Company was among the strongest in circulation (along with Benham and Lynch) and yet from those merchants in Evarts who would take it, these brass tokens fetched but eighty-five cents on the dollar.

The scrip from lesser mines didn't fair even that well. Dad remarks, "We called that ol' scrip at Draper 'floatin' power.' The stuff was so thin and flimsy that it would float! It was made of aluminum. You could bend it in half between your thumb and finger." Outside the Draper camp, "floatin' power" was worth fifty cents on the dollar, if a merchant would take it at all.

The company store at 31 had groceries and some dry goods. It also housed the office of the mining company, which occupied the left side of the building. The office was walled off from the store itself. There was a door for access into the office and an open window framed into the wall at which miners and their family members could transact a cash advance. "Go to the window" was an expression those living in the camps used for getting an advance.

The larger company store at 30, a two-story affair, also had furniture and gas pumps. Purchases, like cash advances, came out of the miner's pay come payday. Larger purchases, a sofa for example, would be dispersed over several paydays. Everything from groceries to clothing and other dry goods to home furnishings were typically bought at the company store (also called a commissary). Company stores purchased goods wholesale but many of them sold to the miners for prices often inflated above retail. This, again, was a way of upping their profit.

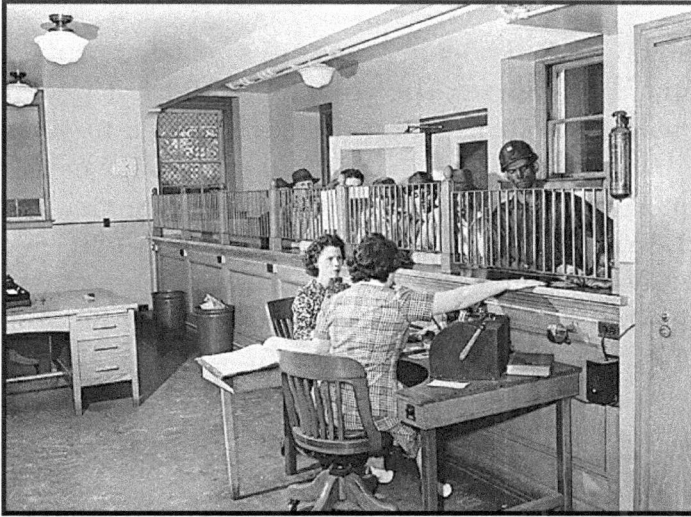

Figure 27. Miners and wives "going to the window" for an advance. (Courtesy National Archives. Used by permission.)

All of this combines to explain what the singer meant when, on behalf of miners everywhere he lamented about owing his soul to the company store.[70]

Dad tells a related story:

These two men approached the mine superintendent, J. J. Asbury, looking for a job. He told 'em, 'We don't have nothin' right now but robbin' work.'[71] ["Robbing" is mining out the coal pillars left in place to support the top while mining the sections. Robbing, also called pulling or drawing, is done only when the particular mine is mined out or is being abandoned for other reasons.] The miners knowed, of course, what he was referrin' to, but they used this chance to make a point. One of 'em said, 'Well, we never did no work in a company store before, but we're willing to give it a try!'

Small independent businesses existed outside the camps[72] of course. The companies did not (technically, anyway) have jurisdiction there. One such business was the "rolling store," of Mr. Hatmaker. I do have one vague memory of a rolling store. I think we were visiting Dollie and Sine, who still lived in Black Mountain. We were already living in Harlan at this time. I remember as a child thinking that the rolling store was just about the coolest thing I had ever seen!

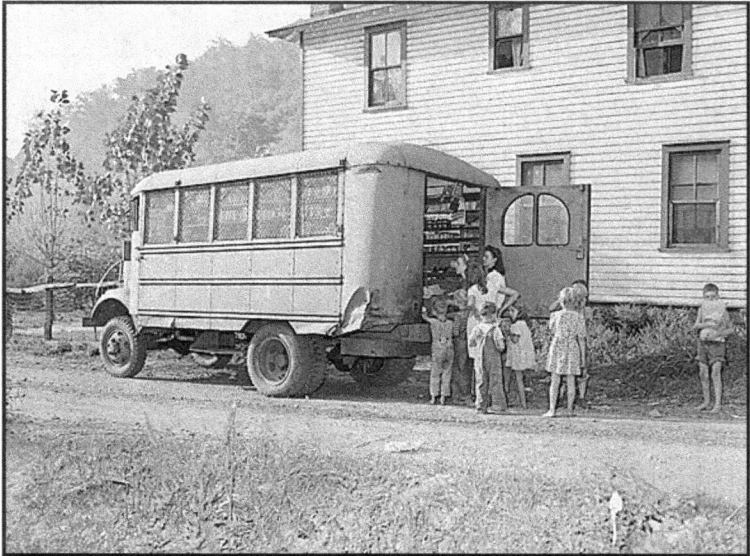

Figure 28. Mr. Hatmaker's rolling store (Courtesy National Archives. Used by permission.)

Mother recalls that Mr. Hatmaker came through every day but Sundays. He had converted an old school bus so that instead of two rows of seats, it had two long rows of shelves. The shelves were divided up, much as they are in quick stops today – candy here, canned goods there, paper goods on down, and so on. "He had about anything you'd want," Mother recalls. She shares a story regarding my sister Pat, that I suspect was true of children all over the camps.

> He circled all around Black Mountain. He would come down the alley in back of our row of houses [now named Bath House Road]. When Pat heard him coming she would say, 'Mother, can I go out to Hatmaker's and get some candy?' Sometimes I'd let her but since we always had sweets in the house, I'd usually say no. Pat would say, 'Well, can I go get you a can of cream? I bet you need a can of cream.' She just wanted to go to Hatmaker's rolling store, of course. Every kid I knew liked to do that. It was something they all enjoyed.

Dad adds a quick story about the guy who came through with his own rolling store after Mr. Hatmaker ceased his operation. He and Mother think his name was Mr. Burton, and that he was from Baxter.

> A feller went to the rollin' store to get a can of cream. 'How much for a can of cream?' he hollers up to Mr. Burton.
>
> 'Fifteen cents,' the man tells him.
>
> The feller says, 'How much for two cans?'
>
> Mr. Burton says, 'Thirty cents.'
>
> Thinkin' he was a-gettin' a bargain that knothead says, 'Oh, well then – I'll take two!'

As I told Mother on one of our trips for this book, I can't imagine the area thriving as she described in those years. "Honey, this place was just alive back then. It's even hard for me to imagine now." To handle the influx of miners, both 30 and 31 alike had three large boarding houses, along with their abundance of company houses and "Official Hollow," where the mining bosses and their families lived.

There was one man in Black Mountain nobody wanted to see. It was not that he was a bad fellow. But in his official capacity, he was not an invited guest to any of the little camp homes that dotted the hollow. Blackie Sexton was his name, and he was a taxi driver. He was good at his job and people liked him in this capacity. Blackie, however, had a secondary job – or task, to put it better – that was as ominous as his primary occupation was benign. It was not a job he liked nor relished. It was the reason no one wanted to see him at their door uninvited.

These were the war years. When a soldier was seriously wounded or killed in action, it was Mr. Sexton's charge to deliver the telegram. "If you saw him getting out of the car and heading to a house, it was so sad," says Mother. "You knew something terrible had happened." I suspect this unwanted task with which Mr. Sexton was charged was a heavy burden to bear.

Aside from the unfortunate families he called on, there was a particular person who hated seeing Mr. Sexton. In fact, this person was haunted every time he saw that taxi coming down the road. I'm speaking of Dad.

Immediately after Pearl Harbor, Dad's intention, like that of many a young man, was to go straight to the recruiting office. But the coal company had deferred Dad, as it did with all those they considered their better workers. As I said earlier, the war needed coal, and coal does not mine itself. The government gave the companies the responsibility of deferring the number of miners necessary to ensure that the critical coal production was maintained.

Dad hated his deferment. For one thing, Japan and Germany had a reckoning coming. He felt strongly that it was his duty, and it was definitely his desire, to help deliver the retribution.

But there was more. Some men pulled any string they could to intentionally get deferred. They wanted nothing to do with military service. These men were roundly considered unpatriotic, cowardly, and were viewed as draft dodgers. Dad wanted no association with this group. Although anybody who knew him knew better, Dad felt linked to these men by his deferment.

The patriotic songs birthed by the war only added to Dad's pain. Songs like *Over There* and *Keep 'em Flying* and *He's 1A in the Army and A1 in My Heart* and *When the Lights Go On Again*, were like goads in the heart to Dad every time he heard one. Especially hard was *Rosie the Riveter*, the basic message being that while the guys were "over there," the women were doing the necessary work here to "keep 'em flying." Dad felt horribly like he wasn't doing his part of the fighting.

When the company deferred me, I went to raisin' Cain about it. Mrs. Stoner [Nellie Stoner, next door neighbor and wife of Oliver] heard me a-cussin' and raisin' Cain. She later come to the fence and asked Della, 'What's wrong with Carl? I

never heard him going on like that.' I was still
mad, buddy. When Della told me that I said, 'Tell
her she never heard of me a-gettin' a deferment
either!'

I went down to the draft board and asked just
what would have happened if I hadn't got that
deferment. The woman there said, 'Well, you'd get
a change in registration and you'd be subject to a
call for a physical examination.'

She was a smart aleck. I guess she thought at
first that I was a-wantin' that deferment. She
didn't know the bondage I was under, buddy. I
didn't want it!

She was a-gettin' kindly cute with me about it
and I said, 'Would you do me a favor? Would you
just forget that I got that deferment? I'll get that
changed!'

Dad's intention was to go back to the company office
and insist they release his deferment. He just couldn't
bear having it. "I wasn't about to be called no draft
dodger! I wasn't wantin' to be no hero or nothin', but I'm
a man that thinks if you won't fight for your country,
you shouldn't be in it!"

Dad was about to be met with what he considered to
be some of the best news he ever got:

Well, that woman's call just about beat me back
home! In a day or two I got reclassified and was
called for an examination. I was to go to
Cincinnati for a physical. So we all got on the
bus, the ones that was to get physicals, and went
to Cincinnati.

Well, we got off the bus at the base there and we
was a-standin' in line, and one of them Black
Mountain cliff apes [explained in Chapter 9]

whistled at some pretty girl who passed by. Well, when he did, this little ol' soldier that was kindly in charge said, 'You'll have to excuse them. They're from Harlan County. They don't know no better!'

That made me mad, buddy. I told him, 'I may be from Harlan County,' but I said, 'I can cram you in that mailbox there!' I said, 'It wasn't becoming of him to whistle like that at that lady but it wasn't right of you to pop off about us either!'

Next time I seen him he was a-cleanin' a commode! He had a little stripe [chevron on his sleeve]. I wasn't in the service yet, you see. I knowed he didn't have no power over me!

I passed that physical in flyin' colors. Man, I was in shape back then! But they cut me on account of my thumb bein' half off [from the first mining accident]. They gave me a 4F on account of my thumb. That killed me. I wanted in the Marines.

Well, I held the line up, Buddy! I went back through. I told the soldier manning that line, 'I want to see that guy again [the doctor].' The doctor was an officer. I told him my thumb didn't hinder me. He said, 'Let's see you grip my hand.' I took him by the hand and clamped down on it. He flinched. He said, 'They ain't a thing wrong with him!'

I said, 'I'll peel potatoes or anything to serve!' He jerked that 'Rejected' out and passed me!

Well, they was takin' the younger men first in the draft you see, and movin' up from there. If they'd a-made one more call-up, I'd a-got to go. But they never made a call for my age group [Dad was 25] for they was so many young men a-volunteerin'.

The war brought rationing at home. Books of designated rationing stamps were meted out for coffee, cornmeal, lard, meat, flour, for most all staples and even some dry goods, like shoes. Wives became adroit at stretching things. For example, to grease a skillet for cornbread, Mother would wipe the skillet with the wax paper the lard was wrapped in. This at once saved the valuable lard and greased the skillet so the bread didn't stick.

Figure 29. Flyer on use of ration stamps during WWII. (Courtesy National Archives. Used by permission.)

Mother says:

The money was flowing but in the war years you had to have the rationing stamps to get your staple goods. You guarded your book of stamps more than your money back then. You could tell when some of the rations were in at the company store. You'd see somebody coming down the track with a bag of goods. We would call out to each other from the porch or the tracks to pass along the news of what had come in [now *that's* social media!].

Rationing coupons were swapped around and shared. This, along with the first generation social media mentioned above were just two more ways in which the communal nature of the camps played out.

Patriotism and anger were running high during the early to mid-1940s. Dad was so infuriated by Pearl Harbor that he made a pass through the house, gathered up everything that was made in Japan, destroyed it, and threw it in the garbage. (This frustrated Mother's practical nature to no end!)

Moreover, this was not a good time to be making nationalistic jokes or anti-American comments. Dad tells this story:

Me, Ott Wynn, Hubert Mulkey and some others was at the Red Store [between 30 and 31]. We had gone in to get us a co-cola. They was some fellers there that wasn't from Black Mountain, and they kept sayin' things to try and agitate us, for some reason. We didn't know any of 'em. They'd been drinkin' and one of 'em was kindly [kind of] leadin' 'em.

I said, 'Buddy, we don't want no trouble here.' Directly, we just walked out of the Red Store to leave and was a-headin' home. They follered us out in a little bit and he – the one that was leadin' 'em – hollered at us. I told them that was with me to go on. I said, 'I'll take care of this.' I turned around and went back.

He said, 'I'm a Jap. What do you think of that!' He wasn't Japanese at all. He was just tryin' to start somethin', for some reason. I said, 'I can't help what you are, but I ain't got no use for no Jap. Why don't you just go on about your business.'

He walked up to me and said somethin' and called me a sonofabitch. When he said that, he took a swing at me. I stepped his swing and as I did, I saw a reflection a-comin' off something in his hand. He had swung at me with a switchblade. When I saw that reflection, I caught him with my left fist, buddy. I hit him so hard I broke the windin' stem off my wristwatch. I thought I'd broke my fist!

When I hit him it knocked him down and I jumped astride him right there on that blacktop. I rared back and caught him on the corner of the chin and knocked him plumb out. I raised him up and he was still a-holdin' that switchblade. I took that knife from him. Later on, a few days later, I give that switchblade to my brother Ed.

When I got up the next mornin' and was puttin' on my overalls, my leg went plumb through the belly of 'em. That feller, I didn't know it at the time, but he had cut my overalls from here to here [completely across the belly region]. I wasn't even scratched, but my overalls was cut wide open. Buddy, that made me mad!

Turns out the provocateur and his friends were from Pine Mountain. Relevant to his "Jap" comment and to add to the poignancy of this story is the fact that this altercation occurred on the evening of August 14, 1945...VJ Day. This was not the time for the stranger from Pine Mountain to try to impress anyone with his booze-fueled bombast. Dad remarks:

I heard later that he was supposed to be a bad man. I didn't think he was nothin' but unpatriotic and a dirty coward – goin' on with all that Jap business and then pickin' a fight and comin' at an unarmed man with a switchblade!

As I said, this skirmish occurred on the grand evening of VJ Day, August 14, 1945. To the relief of everyone, the war was now over.

Coal-yard Facts

The largest coal-producing state in America is Wyoming, producing 39% of the nation's coal.

CHAPTER 9

Dadspeak

Dad had a rich lexicon of terms, phrases, and sayings. By no means did all of them originate with him, though many did. Regardless of their source, Dad was extremely adroit in their application and use. The following are some of my favorite examples of Dadspeak.

» *He's so dumb he'd swim a river to get a drink of water*
There's dumb and then there's "you can't fix stupid" dumb. This expression is reserved for the latter. For example, a woman got on the bus at a bus stop and stepping up to the driver she said, "Mary Alice." This meant she was going to Mary Alice (south of Harlan), and the driver then told her the charge.

A friend of Dad's stepped up behind her to board the bus and, thinking he was following the woman's example, said "Johnny Hanson." The poor soul thought the woman was giving the driver her name, so he did likewise. That's "swim a river to get a drink dumb." [By the way, the man's name is changed for what I trust is an obvious reason.]

» *He's so crooked he'll have to be screwed in the ground when he dies*

For the incorrigible among us.

» *He wouldn't hit at a snake*

A reference to the individual who has raised laziness to an art form. The idea is that even if a viper were crawling on him, he wouldn't put forth the effort to knock it off.

» *No account*

No good, of no value. Used to describe an individual who is, in the vernacular, worthless.

"Buddy, I've knowed that feller for many a year and I can tell you he's no account."

» *I can remember when you could go to the store and get ten cents worth of bacon. Why, today they wouldn't wipe the stain off the knife for ten cents!*

» *I wouldn't swap nickels with him*

For the wheeler dealer, the man who could sell snow to an Eskimo. The idea is that if you traded such a man one nickel for another, he would figure out some way to make a profit.

» *It's a long road that ain't got a curve in it*

Don't get cocky when you're riding high. You won't always be on top, so brace yourself because the hard times will come in some fashion, as they do to all.

Also used to mean, don't think you're getting away with anything. It will catch up to you eventually, because we reap what we sow.

» *Pick and pluck*

To pester or bother. The image is that of picking and plucking feathers from a chicken in preparation for cooking it.

Dad was about the most ticklish man I have ever seen. I liked to sneak up behind him and tickle him just to watch him half jump out of his shoes. Dad would jokingly say something like "Why don't you leave me alone, you pickin' and pluckin' thing!"

» *Smart*

Not what you probably think. In Southern Appalachia, "smart" often carries the connotation of hard working.

"I tell you what, buddy. I liked working together with ol' Jim. He was one of the smartest fellers that worked at 31."

» *Mortly*

This is a contraction of "mortally." The word is probably more familiar to the reader as being associated with death (e.g., mortally wounded). But the term has a second meaning which is "intensely, earnestly, or seriously." This is the usage Dad had in mind when he employed, as he often did, "mortly."

"Buddy, when that boar hog pulled out from under the front of the T Model you should have seen him take off. That thing was mortly flyin' when it lit out across them tracks!"

» *Straighten up and fly right*

This is one we kids would hear from time to time! It means, "get your act together" or "stop misbehaving." It comes from a popular 1944 song by the Nat King Cole Trio named, appropriately enough, *Straighten Up and Fly Right*.

» *Knothead*

The hardest part of any wood, natural or milled, is a knot. So someone who is a knothead is hard headed. Dad also used it to imply stubborn or foolish, and always in a comical and good-natured sense. "When that knothead heard that one can of cream cost 15 cents and two cost 30 cents, he thought he was a-gettin' a bargain by buyin' two of 'em!"

» *Lathered up*

Sounds like it has something to do with shaving, doesn't it? Well, indirectly that's true. "Lathered up" means to be very angry. The rural expression for a rabid dog is "mad dog." A rabid animal foams at the mouth and thus looks "lathered up," as though ready for a shave. So, when someone gets very angry ("mad") he is said to be lathered up. "Lord have mercy, did Joe get lathered up when he found out he'd lost his carbide out of that hole in his back pocket!"

» *That don't favor nothin'*

This one never failed to make me chuckle. When Dad saw something that looked weird or he had been working on something that didn't initially turn out like he wanted, he would invoke "That don't favor nothin'!" A literal translation would be, "That doesn't look like anything."

» *Plug ugly*

The Plug Uglies originated in Baltimore, Maryland in the mid-1800s. Basically they were a street gang. So when someone was referred to as a "plug ugly," the implication is that they were someone of a villainous nature. "I told that plug ugly he better leave us alone and go about his business."

» *Of a-mornin' or of a-evenin'*

An Irish expression still used in that country today. In fact, I heard it numerous times on a recent trip there. Dad used these phrases regularly, especially in connection to fishing or hunting. "We'd get up early of a-mornin' so we could be in the woods when the sun come up."

» *Smotherin'*

The only sad example of *Dadspeak* I've included. This was a term every mining region in Southern Appalachia is familiar with. Smotherin' (smothering) was the term given to the difficulty in breathing miners with respiratory conditions – most extremely, black lung – experienced. Many times I've heard Dad say, "I had to get up and sleep in my chair last night. I was havin' a hard time sleepin' because I took a smotherin' spell."

» *He'd wear a straw hat to a Christmas tree*

A description of the naïve, or those lacking in good judgment and insight. Straw hats are for the summer, Christmas trees, the winter. Showing up at Christmas time in a straw hat implies being ill equipped for life.

» *That feller would suck eggs*

To get this one, you have to understand another country saying, "egg-sucking dog." Some dogs develop the taste for eggs. They sneak into the henhouse, crack open the eggs and suck (lap, actually) the egg from the shell. This not only takes food from the farmer's table, it also takes money from his pocket (if he sells eggs or raises chickens to sell). If ever a dog develops a taste for eggs, he won't give up the habit until the farmer intervenes. (In the 1941 court case, Hull v. Scruggs, the Mississippi Supreme Court actually ruled on just such a case. Mr. Scruggs killed the dog of Mr. Hull because the latter's dog was raiding his hen house and "sucking eggs." The court ruled in favor of Mr. Scruggs.)

So, to call a person an "egg sucking dog" or to say of a person he would "suck eggs" is a strong term of derision. It means the person is a "weasel" (another egg sucker, by the way), a sneaky, underhanded individual who will do just about anything. It means the person is untrustworthy, will take any advantage to further himself with no concern for others, etc.

» *Looking like Ned in the First Reader*

A reference to the famous *McGuffey Readers*, the series of primers dating back to 1836, and still in use today in many circles. We are told in the Eclectic Primer (studied before the First Reader) that Ned did not like school, therefore he did not apply himself. So, when he got to the First Reader his reading skills were lacking. The implication is that he would just stare at the page and not have a clue as how to read the text before him. (In the Fourth Primer there is a poem, *Lazy Ned*, that ends by saying that when Ned got to the end of his life he "died a dunce at last.")

172

So, to "look like Ned in the First Reader" means to be looking at something in front of you and to be unsure how to proceed, to be confused, uncertain. It means to be lost, or to be staring at something (usually accompanied by a blank expression) like you don't have a clue.

For example, "Marvin couldn't read a map any more than he could read Chinese, buddy. He just set there on the side of the road starin' at it, looking like Ned in the First Reader, a-tryin' to make sense of it."

» *A circus dog couldn't jump over it*

Used to emphasize a great amount of something. The implication is that even a dog trained to perform (a "circus dog") couldn't jump high or far enough to clear the heap. "Mom and Della had cooked so much food a circus dog couldn't jump over it."

» *Richer than churn cream*

Sweet cream (or whole milk) was poured into the churn and then churned to make butter. It is quite rich, of course. To be "richer than churn cream" is to either have a lot of money or at least give the appearance of having a lot of money. "He may not have had a penny to his name, I don't know. But the way he was dressed he looked richer than churn cream!"

» *Laying all jokes aside*

Implying that what is about to be said is to be taken seriously. As in, "Laying all jokes aside, we had better leave by four o'clock if we intend to be there by seven."

It's interesting how expressions wafted into the hills over time from more "sophisticated" origins. This expression is from the Irish playwright and politician

Richard Brinsley Sheridan (1751 – 1816). It is found in "The Money-Hunter" from his play "The Duenna" in which Isaiah says to Jerome, "Don Jerome, come now, let us lay aside all joking, and be serious."

» *Buddy, I was so poor durin' the Depression that if eggs was sellin' for a dime a dozen, I couldn't buy the echo off a cackle!*

» *It's a thousand wonders*

A wonder is something that is remarkable, amazing, astonishing. If one wonder is amazing, imagine what a thousand wonders all rolled into one must be! Dad used this expression for emphasis. "Boys I'll tell you what's the truth. It's a thousand wonders some of us wasn't hurt bad when that man trip crashed!"

» *That ain't bad on one winding*

If you're under 40 you may not know this but wristwatches used to have to be wound daily – which is why they had a "winding stem" – or they would run down and stop. If you're 50 or older you will remember this experience: You or someone with you looks at their watch, sees that it has the wrong time and says "Oh, I forgot to wind my watch!" Remember that?

When Dad would remark "that's not bad for one winding," it meant that he got a good outcome for what had been put into it. "We caught 15 catfish on the first baitin' of that trotline. That ain't bad on one windin'!"

» *Older than black pepper*

Dad often used this one on himself in his later years. "Boys I'll tell you what's the truth, I've never heard of such as that in my entire life, and I'm older than black pepper!"

» *Take hog-rifle sights*

The fastest and most efficient way to dispatch a hog, come butchering time, was a single shot to the forehead, equidistant to and just above the eye line. The weapon of choice was a .22 rifle and the men who were good at it prided themselves on being able to drop the hog cleanly. The skull of a hog is quite hard to penetrate (you've heard of "pig headed," right?). An inferior shot would often just glance off and addle the animal – and no one wants to be around a four-hundred-pound addled hog! Or, the animal could be wounded in a mortal fashion, but one which results in three or four minutes of mayhem before it died. Messy.

So, to take "hog-rifle sights" means to be precise, to make accuracy your primary intent, to pay attention to what you are doing. Anyone, for example, sawing a board needs to "take hog-rifle sights" at what they are doing, so they don't cut the board too short.

» *So contrary that if he fell in a river he'd float upstream*

A description of an obstinate, stubborn or oppositional person. Someone who wants to be different just for different's sake. Someone who would bury himself alive just to prove to everyone he knows how to use a shovel.

» *They'll hang him when his ass gets heavy enough to break his neck*

Used to describe a youngster who looks like pure trouble. Someone who, unless they change their ways, has very little future.

» *The soles of my shoes was so thin durin' the Depression that if I stepped on a dime I could tell you if it was heads or tails!*

» It's a rich man's war and a poor man's fight

This was used in both a literal and a metaphorical sense. Literally, it's well known that the sons of the wealthy have always had means of avoiding military service that the poor man did not. During the Civil War, for example, the Conscription took immigrant men (mostly from Ireland) straight to the military. Men living in New York could buy themselves out of the draft for $300.00. None of the poor could afford to do this, of course.

Metaphorically it is used to mean that men of wealth may get the ball rolling but ultimately, it all rolls downhill and it is the poor who pay the price.

» Mealy-mouthed

A description for someone who is afraid of speaking frankly or reticent to speak in a direct, straightforward manner when called for.

In his frustration, Dad often accused Mother of having this attribute when it appeared as if someone spoke to her inappropriately [In Dad's absence, of course!] and she didn't stand up for herself. He'd get miffed at her and say, "Della, you're just too mealy-mouthed!"

» Sergeant York's overcoat wouldn't make him a smokin' jacket

Those who don't know their history might not get this one. Sergeant York was a Tennessee boy who was a Medal of Honor recipient and famous WWI hero. A smoking jacket was a garment worn by men in the Victorian house for leisure (often while smoking a pipe or cigar).

The idea is that the great Sergeant's overcoat wouldn't be deemed good enough for such a man to just wear around the house relaxing. That is to say, this is a person who is completely full of himself. People often say of someone like this, "I'd like to buy him for what he's worth and sell him for what he thinks he's worth!"

» *Lily livered*

To be "lily livered" is to be a coward or to act in a cowardly fashion. Here is an example from Dad and some friends who were out one evening: "When them fellers from Highsplint jumped us, ol' J. T., who should have been a-helpin' us, was nowhere to be found. Turns out that lily-livered thing had hid in behind the jukebox, buddy!"

Before the modern era it was believed that four bodily fluids ("humors") governed personality. One of these, yellow bile, was believed to govern the cluster of emotions like boldness, courage, and anger. One who lacked sufficient yellow bile, a deficit which was believed to cause the liver to be pale or white in color (like a lily), lacked these personality traits. Thus, such a person would be cowardly, timid, fearful. This person was called "lily-livered" or "white-livered."

Who says Black Mountain lacked erudition and sophistication? Why, Dad and others who used this expression were actually quoting Shakespeare! "Go prick thy face and over-red thy fear, thou lily livered boy." (Macbeth 5:3:17)

» *Too deeper read* [pronounced as the past-tense verb with a short e – sounds like "red"]

Employed when someone is speaking on some subject not understood by or over the head of the listener. For example:

> Some of 'em was up on Ivy Hill [Not the more familiar Ivy Hill in Harlan. This Ivy Hill was on a mountaintop up in a hollow in 31, and was also called "Poker Knob."] playing poker and drinkin' and one of 'em got to talkin' about somethin' way over the head of Ike [a friend of Dad's]. That feller asked Ike what he thought about what he had just said. Ike said, 'Hell buddy, I don't even know what you're talking about. You're too deeper read for me!'

» *Come within a pea of*

A pea is a tiny thing, so to "come within a pea" is to cut something close, come very close. "I come within a pea of fallin' out-a that boat, buddy!"

» *Don't get above your raisin'*

Do not become haughty or develop an air of superiority relative to the people and places you grew up with or around. (It does not mean don't try to better yourself, of course.)

» *High on the hog*

I suppose everyone has heard this one, but do you know its socioeconomic origin and significance? The rich ate shoulder roasts, loins, chops, proper bacon, and hams – those cuts of meat that are, literally, high up on the hog's body. The poor ate from the lower parts of the hog – the trotters (feet), fatback, chitterlings ("chitlins"), and so on. Other parts of the hog and trimmings were ground together to make sausage. So if you "ate high on the hog tonight," you had a meal consisting of finer food.

A TV commercial used to run in Knoxville in which a sausage company boasted that their sausage was made of the "finest cuts of hams, shoulders, and loins." This commercial agitated Dad to no end. "Them people are either liars or fools. Who in the world would take hams and shoulders and loins and grind 'em for sausage!" Sausage is a "low on the hog" food. It is made from the ground trimmings from the animal.

(Dad raised and butchered one hog a year for the family. He was quite skilled at the task and others called on him to butcher their hogs for them. His fee was one tenderloin per hog. Dad always said, "If you butcher your hog right there ain't nothin' left to throw away but the squeal.")

The term "high on the hog" is also used metaphorically to mean rich, or the pretense of wealth. "Man, they're living high on the hog!"

» *Duke's mixture*

"Duke's mixture" was a makeshift tobacco blend that an actual Southern (North Carolina) farmer named Duke scraped together from what the Yankee army left of his crop, after they had either destroyed or stolen nearly everything on his farm. The phrase as typically used means a less than exquisite or a rag-tag mixture of things.

For example, I love Thai food. When Mother (remember, the world's pickiest eater) sees me with a nice plate of yellow curry or pa nang she will usually look at it, squint her nose and say, "Shooo goodness. What in the world is that Duke's mixture?"

» *Study on it*

This and the next one are my two favorites. To "study on it" means to think something through, to solve a problem. Dad used this expression and the next one quite frequently. "I'm gonna study on that a bit before I get to work on it," would be a typical Dad saying.

A variant of this expression often used by Dad is "think on it a spell."

» *Cliff ape*

There's just something about this one that I love. It never fails to strike me as such a funny expression! I think a lot of that has to do with the fact that I can remember how Dad would use it, and the way he would tell those stories in which he employed it.

A cliff ape is a mountain man from way back in the hollow who doesn't characteristically stray far from his territory, and to put it mildly, is not exactly cosmopolitan. "Rube" would be an adequate synonym. "That cliff ape just pulled out his pistol, buddy, and shot a hole plumb through the theater screen!"

It morphed over time to mean a knucklehead or someone whose behavior was inappropriate to the situation.

To illustrate, Dad had a friend from back in one of the hollows who bought a new pair of "dress shoes." They were a bit snug and he asked Dad what he could do to remedy that. Dad told him to lace the shoes up, pack them with dried beans as full as possible, and leave them overnight. This action would stretch the leather a bit. Dad tells the outcome:

Well, he got up the next morning buddy and the uppers of both shoes had busted loose all the way 'round. The leather busted right apart from the stitchin' to the soles! He come over and showed 'em to me. I'd never seen anything like it! I asked him what in the world he had done.

I said, 'Did you do it just like I told you?'

He said, 'Yeah, I laced 'em up, packed 'em as full of beans as I could, wet 'em good, and set 'em to stretch overnight, just like you told me.'

I said, 'Wet 'em? I didn't say nothin' about wettin' the beans!'

He said, 'Well Carl, you always soak beans before you cook 'em!'

I said, 'Lord have mercy, what did cookin' beans have to do with this?!'

That cliff ape had soaked them beans, buddy. Well they went to expandin' you see, overnight, and somethin' had to give! It give alright. Both shoe tops give completely loose from the soles!

Then there is this one. A friend of Dad's was walking the road from 31 to 30 (an altogether common practice then). Someone driving by stopped and asked the man if he wanted a ride (again, very common). The fellow replied, "No thanks. I'm in a hurry." Cliff ape.

I remember Dad's terminology as fondly as I do his stories given, among other reasons, that the two are so intertwined. His expressions were used in his stories and I can't imagine the one without the other.

Coal-yard Facts

Scientists tell us it takes from three to seven feet of compacted plant matter to form one foot of bituminous coal.

CHAPTER 10

An Iron-Strong Woman

Della Vaughn was born the second of four daughters to Henry and Laura Vaughn. Both parents were descendants of English settlers. Her mother was a Sams by birth, and they hailed from the English settlement of Sams Gap, North Carolina.

Mother was delivered by Doc Lewis, and her entrance into this world was very nearly followed by her immediate exit from it. Mother tells the story:

> Mom [my grandmother, Laura] said when I came out my face was blue-black and there was very little sign of life. Mom had a very hard labor and Doc Lewis told my Dad he didn't know if he could save both of us.
>
> Dad said, 'Well, I don't want to lose either of them but if it comes down to it, save Laura. We have another girl to raise [Goldie] and she's going to need her mother. I can't raise her without Laura.'
>
> There was a Mrs. Vanover there, Nancy Vanover. I think she was a relative of some sorts. [She was

the mother of Walter Vanover, whom you will read about shortly.] Doc Lewis had laid me on the other side of the bed while he worked with Mom. He told Mrs. Vanover to watch me close and look for any signs of life. I gasped at some point and moved a little. Mrs. Vanover called to Doc Lewis and he came over and began to work with me. Doc Lewis pulled me through.

I was kind of puny until I was about twelve. I was so skinny my shoulder blades stuck out. Dollie and Goldie both were heavier than me.

The toughness and resilience Mother showed at birth would demonstrate itself time and again throughout her life. She came into this world as she lives to this day – iron strong. Mother is something of a conundrum. If you met her (as anyone who knows her will testify), the words that would come to mind are caring, kind, gentle, loving, patient, tender, calm. She is conflict avoidant and sensitive to a fault, and she knows it.

I will tell you though – and there is no hyperbole here, nor am I seeing this through the idealizing eyes of her son – Mother is perhaps the strongest person I know. The things she has been through would have consumed a weaker person.

In addition to her birth experience, Mother faced two significant traumatic ordeals during her childhood. The first of these ordeals was the previously discussed Battle of Evarts. Mother says:

We were ready for school. Mom went to [Jim] Turner's grocery to get something. I don't recall what. She told us not to leave for school until she got back. She came back and said, 'You're not going to school today. Mr. Turner said not to let you go. There's going to be trouble in Evarts.'

About that time we started to see people go down Snuff Street with guns and down the riverbank with guns. They were all heading toward the bell crossing. [It is interesting to me to realize that during the Battle of Evarts, Mother was above the bell crossing at the same time that Dad – whom she did not know at the time – was below it.]

Then the shooting started. We all hid in our farthest bedroom, behind the fireplace. Goldie was so scared, she tried to stick her head up the chimney to hide! Oh God, could we hear the shooting! We could hear bullets hitting everywhere. It sounded like they were hitting our house.

There was a man, Mr. Ball, up the street on Snuff Street who ran a garage. [This is the same garage in which Dad took his union vows, mentioned earlier.] He opened the doors to let us run up the ramp into the garage for safety, then he shut the doors.

The shooting kind of ceased for a bit. We ran through the garage and into a block building owned by the Powell brothers, Raleigh and Ben. They had a store on the first floor and lived on the second. They got us into a bathroom there to protect us. Their mother, Mrs. Powell, was there too. [Mother recalls the Powell brothers had two sisters, both of whom were school teachers. 'One was Mint and the other, Betty. They taught school at Evarts.']

We could see men with guns on top of the Roslyn Theater in Evarts. We could see gun barrels sticking out all down through the top of that building, and on other buildings too. I remember seeing so many gun barrels. We was all scared to death. Dad was at work and we were worried about him, but we were also wishing he was there with us to take care of us. Dad left his car at the Kildav mine where he worked, and he walked around the mountain to get home to us. [Attempting to drive home would have taken him through the very heart of the battle.] Many of the miners walked that way back and forth to work at Kildav, but Dad usually drove.

When Dad got home he was scared to death. He thought we'd all been killed because none of us were home! At the time, we lived in the bottom between Main Street and the river in Evarts. I guess Mr. Ball told him where we were. We were all so glad to see each other! We didn't know if he was alive and he didn't know if we were alive!

Dad took us to Uncle Johnny and Aunt Betty Jackson's [Betty Jackson was my grandfather Henry's only sister]. They lived in Evarts too but towards Bailey's Creek, further away from the trouble. I remember that Goldie kept crying and screaming when it was all going on. Me, I couldn't quit laughing. I know that sounds weird but I couldn't make myself stop laughing! [She is describing a psychological phenomenon called hysterical laughter – a response to acute stress exhibited by some.]

I remember that for two or three nights you could see the lights of men walking back and forth through the mountains. You could see the lights of their flashlights and lanterns. That was so spooky. Your mind just run wild with thoughts of what might be going on.

My [maternal] cousin, Lee Logsdon, was staying with us at the time and was working at Kildav mine, with Dad. Lee didn't work the day of the Battle of Evarts, for some reason. As it turns out, he went to his girlfriend Maggie's house, which was on Snuff Street too, not real far from Mr. Ball's garage. [Though uncertain, Mother thinks Maggie's maiden name might have been Brock.] He stayed with her during all that shooting instead of coming back to take care of Mom and us three girls! Dad was so mad when he found out about this that he put him out of the house.

I remember that the kids that had gone to school were sent home on the train, the passenger train. They made them lay on the floor of the train cars for safety, in case the gun thugs shot into the cars.

I don't know how long it lasted but it seemed like hours. I remember when it was over seeing a hole in the road about three feet across. Something that the gun thugs had thrown or shot had exploded and blew a hole in the road. It was on Snuff Street, right there where that short one-way street [state road 215] starts.

Mother was ten years old at the time.

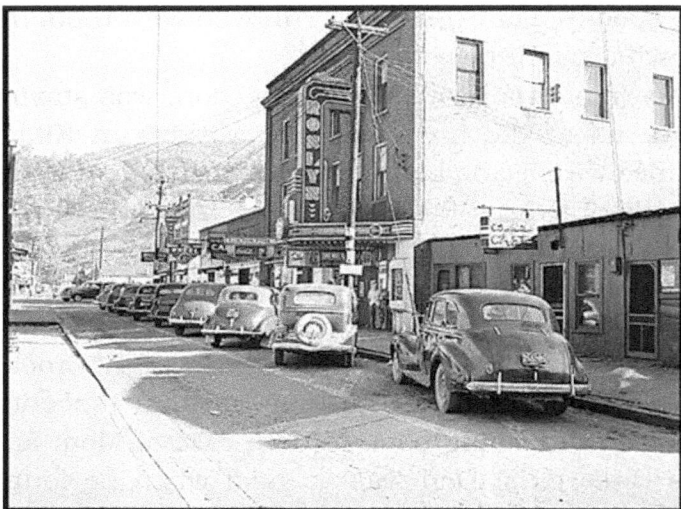

Figure 30. Roslyn Theater in Evarts. The young Della Vaughn saw miners with rifles atop this and other buildings during the Battle of Evarts. (Courtesy National Archives. Used by permission.)

In Evarts recently, Mother and I had a serendipitous encounter at the adjoining Turner and Burkhart cemeteries that ties back to her life the day of the Battle of Evarts. We met a most delightful motorcycle rider, Jim Wallace, and talked to him for some time. Mr. Wallace was visiting the graves of kin in the Turner Cemetery. It turns out he is the nephew of the Jim Turner who owned the grocery store in Evarts, the same Jim Turner who warned Laura Vaughn not to let her girls go to school on the day of the Battle of Evarts.

(While talking, Mr. Wallace shared an anecdote with us that tells me the love of a good story is still alive and well in Harlan County. He says:

A cousin of mine recently died. He was crossing the road to go to the bank when a man driving by whipped a U turn and, not seeing my cousin, ran flat over him and killed him. Turns out, he was my cousin's doctor. How's that for irony. You go to your doctor to get healthy. You don't expect him to kill you!)

––––––––––––––––

A twelve year-old, fifth-grade girl is walking home from school on a grand Thursday late in September, with her best friend, Lora Troglen. The year is 1933. When they get to Nell Smith's café in downtown Evarts (on "the world's shortest one-way street"), a familiar car parked out front causes the girl, Della, to look in the window. Inside is her father, Henry, who at that very moment is sitting at the café counter, taking a chance on a punchboard to win a clock.

The waitress tells Henry to turn around and look at the window. He smiles and waves as the young girl peering through the window is doing likewise. Della then turns and, with her friend, walks on home. Her father turns back around on his stool facing the waitress and says, "That's the one I'm trying to win this clock for."

This is, for all practical purposes, the last time father and daughter will ever see each other.

Della goes home, changes out of her school clothes, and she and her younger sister Dollie go out to play with friends on Snuff Street. The two young sisters see their dad drive across the Evarts Bridge and Della says to Dollie, "There goes Poppa to meet the six o'clock train." (Henry was running a taxi service at the time, while recovering from a mining accident.) It is about 5:45 in the afternoon.

Two piercing gunshots shortly shatter the girls' play. They will, minutes later, shatter their young hearts. Twelve-year-old Della and ten-year-old Dollie run down to their house in the bottom near the river, just below Snuff Street. "I remember that Mom and Goldie was sitting on the front porch peeling potatoes for supper." Mother recalls thinking, at that tender age, "Oh Lord, please don't let it be Poppa!" She tells me, "I just had the strangest feeling that it was him." She was right.

The chronology is this. On his way to the train station, Henry had stopped in the nearby jewelry shop, owned by W. A. Heathen, to pick up a watch he was having repaired. The shop lay just across the Evarts bridge. While in there, an argument of some sort erupted, the details of which are unknown.

Henry (Grandpa), and Walter Vanover, his nephew who was in the car with him, had come back across the bridge to home. (Walter was the son of Martha Vanover, present at Mother's birth, as described earlier.) Uncharacteristically, Henry parked not in front of the house as normal, but rather up the road a ways, in front of the drugstore. He waited in the car as Walter walked nonchalantly down to the house and came back shortly, eating an apple. He called up to the sisters, who were still playing up the road with their friends, and said, "Your Momma said to tell you supper will be ready in a little while." Only later would the family discover why Walter came back to the house. He had come to get Henry's pistol.

Henry and Walter drove back across Evarts Bridge to the jewelry store. For the second time, the two young sisters playing on Snuff Street saw their Daddy's car cross Evarts Bridge. In mere moments, shots rang out. The jeweler was ready. The moment Henry and Walter walked through the door, there was gunplay. Henry was struck under the right armpit. The bullet pierced his lung and lodged just beneath the skin in his back.

Another nephew of Henry's, Ernest Lewis, worked at a nearby "filling station" (which still exists). Someone told him that his Uncle Henry had just been shot. Ernest ran to the jewelry store. He and Walter put Henry in the car and sped off to the hospital. "We could see the car," says Mother. "We didn't know what was going on, but boy, that car was moving on. Ernest was flying!"

"My best friend, Lora Troglen, (who lived across Evarts Bridge, opposite the jewelry store) came running down Snuff Street. She told me my Dad had just been shot." Laura and Goldie must have suspected this because they came up from the house just as Lora told Della and Dollie the news. Della told her mother and Goldie. Laura and her three daughters collapsed in grief and shock into one-another's arms. Lora told them Ernest said he would be back soon "to get Laura and the girls," and for her to run and tell them this.

True to his word, Ernest did return from the Harlan Hospital (Mound Street) to get Laura and the girls. He immediately drove them to the hospital. Laura, Goldie, and Dollie went up to the bed. Della could not. She stood at the door, looking in. "I just couldn't make myself walk up to that bed. I was a Daddy's girl." The dying Henry looked up, smiled, and said, "There are my blue-eyed girls." (All five members of the Vaughn family were blue eyed.) This was the last thing they would ever hear their father say. Della was out of range, and did not hear it.

Dr. Cawood told us that Ernest was going to take us home. He said, 'Your Dad's going to be alright. You can come back in the morning.' We never saw Dad again. He died that night. Dr.

Cawood shouldn't have told us that. I know what he was trying to do, but he shouldn't have told us Poppa was going to be alright.

Aunt Betty Jackson, Dad's only sister, stayed at the hospital that night with Momma. Goldie was fifteen, I was twelve, and Dollie was ten. Our cousin, Henrietta [Johnny and Betty Jackson's oldest daughter], who was older than Goldie, was with us at home. It was Henrietta, and Goldie, Dollie, and me. We three girls [the sisters] stayed huddled up together in the bed all night. Real late, Mom and Aunt Betty came in. They were in pieces. Poppa was dead.

My grandfather, Henry C. Vaughn, whom I never would have a chance to know, died on September 21, 1933. He is buried in the A. R. Dyche Memorial Park, in London, Kentucky. He was thirty-four years old when he was killed, three weeks shy of his thirty-fifth birthday.

In the days following the funeral, Laura and her daughters would move from Evarts[73] to East Bernstadt, to be near Laura's kin. They would later return to Evarts, Laura having bought a house on Evarts Hill. Time would move on, but the young Laura (in her thirties) would never remarry. Her answer when asked about that over and over in the years to come was always the same. "Henry was my man."

These events from childhood – her close call with death at birth, the traumas of the Battle of Evarts and the sudden death of her "Poppa" – were hard, but more hard days lay ahead. Mother's strength would be both tested and fortified time and again in her adult years.

192

The near constant challenges Mother faced from the late 1930s to about 1965 were herculean. Only by the grace of God, her faith, and the support of her family (specifically Mom, and Dollie and Sine), did she make it. Those supports and her indomitable spirit, that is.

I discussed earlier the dynamic opposites within Dad's personality. No greater example of this polarity exists than that between his ever-ready helping nature and amazing sense of humor and love of laughter on the one hand, and his temper on the other. Dad could get madder than any human being I have ever seen. Really. Further, Dad's anger had no stages. There was no simmer or rolling boil stage with him. He went from calm to full-bore rage in the blink of an eye. Dad says, "I used to tell Della I'd rather get sick than get mad." Mother validates that as Dad speaks and adds, "Often Carl would get so mad he *would* get sick." That temper brought a lot of stress into Mother's life in the old days. It was not that Dad had a pattern of physical abuse of Mother or the children. In fact, he never once spanked any of the four of us. The stress to Mother came from worrying over what Dad might do to others when provoked, or what others might have to do to him to defend themselves. Dad had the temper of gunpowder.

From the late 1930s to the mid-1960s, Dad was, as I said earlier, equal parts Good Samaritan and Billy Hell rolled into one form. He was all light and darkness, wisdom and folly, mirth and anger, discipline and defiance, faith and rebellion and somehow he seemed to possess each of these attributes in full. In short, he was like all of us, only more so.

Mother and Dad were married on August 13, 1938, and before their journey together is over, they will be married for 58 years, until death parts them. (Dad died February 4, 1997.) Never were two people more unalike in all the land! Psychologically, I suspect that, on a subconscious level, Mother was marrying strength and Dad was marrying goodness.

In 1938, no miner's wife had a serene life. Even if her man was not involved in the union strife, or had a wild streak in him, there was anxiety aplenty. Mine safety was nowhere near where it is today and neither was the company's interest in a miner's welfare. At most mines profit margins, not safety, drove decision making. Every morning a miner's wife woke to see her husband off to a job from which he might not return at shift's end.

With Dad, everything was amped up. If there was a picket, Dad was there. If there was a conflict, he'd be in the thick of it. Dad began party drinking during the Coxton years, and he was not one of those mellowed by the effects of alcohol. Mother says, "Anytime Carl went out the door, I never knew if I'd see him again because of what might happen when he was out. It kept me on edge all the time."

It wasn't that Dad was continually rowdy. Not by any means. To the contrary, one would have a difficult time finding any man who took certain of his responsibilities more seriously. It's just that in addition to this responsible side, Dad had a wild and reckless nature in those days. Mother remarks, "It's like he never realized it wasn't just him anymore. He had a wife now, and later, kids to think about. It's like he never got that." If there was a dangerous job that needed doing in the mine, he would volunteer. If there was something hazardous in a picket strife, he wanted to handle it. If trouble broke out with some toughs from another area, he would be right in the thick of it. The more dangerous the situation, the more comfortable Dad seemed to be.

For example, Mother and Dad had a friend and neighbor in 31 Camp named Fat Taylor. I do not know Mr. Taylor's first name, everyone knew him as "Fat."

Fat Taylor lived across the road from Mother and Dad in Black Mountain. He kept a few hogs for meat. He had his hog pen on a rise which was close to Yocum Creek (a branch off the Clover Fork River). The creek flooded (as it frequently did before the redirect in Harlan, several years ago), and Fat's hogs were trapped by the rising water. Their drowning was imminent. Dad says:

> I had to go in there and get them hogs for Fat. Man, that water was a-ragin'. I'd go in the water there above Fat's house and where I'd come out would be down at Brittians Creek Bridge. The water was that swift. It was hairy, buddy! I was able to save two of Fat's hogs.

I said to Dad, "How did you get into that situation? Did you think the hogs were worth the risk to your life?" He answered, "I was just that way, honey. I'd do anything I could to help a man."

And that was true. That was absolutely true about Dad, as anyone who knew him would attest. It was also true, though, that Dad was drawn to the dangerous. It is as if that was his natural environment. Note the words Dad used in his statement above. "I *had to* get in there and get them hogs, for Fat." He really felt that way about it! He felt it was his obligation to help anyone in need. That was his nature. Still, this is an example of how he often jeopardized his wellbeing, neglecting completely how Mother was affected by these behaviors.

Regarding the crisis with Mr. Taylor's hogs, Mother says:

I remember I had been to the company store at 30 to do some shopping. When I got back home I heard that Carl had been in that river to save some hogs. That just floored me, because the river was way up and was moving fast. I said, 'Carl, what on earth were you thinking! What would have become of us if you'd drowned?!'

Carl said, 'Well Della, I had to get them hogs of Fat's or they would have drowned!'

That is how he thought. I don't say that as praise. I think antics of this sort were terribly unwise and, as Mother says, thoughtless in some ways. He had a wife and children to think of. He had responsibilities, and those by no means involved the responsibility to save some guy's porcine possessions. That is just the way he was. (As an aside, I cannot imagine the physical strength it took to rescue two panicked hogs while simultaneously navigating the torrent of a flooded creek!)

Mother faced many a worried night when Dad was out with his friends, on those nights when the wives or girlfriends were left at home. Rowdy men and alcohol do not a good combination make.

Do you recall the story in Chapter 7 about the poker game gone awry at "Nigger John's" house? There is a backstory that I didn't include in the telling. The year 1942 is just a few months old when Mother answers a knock at the door that night.

Blab Davis was standing there. 'Della, Carl told me to come and get his shotgun.' This was way up in the nighttime. I said, 'Lord have mercy Blab, what for?!' He told me about the trouble with Nigger John at the card game. I was so shocked by this because Carl and John was such good friends. It just blew my mind. I begged Blab not to take it. He said, 'Della I have to. You know what Carl will be like if I go back without it!'

Carl had a new shotgun [.16 gauge Remington automatic, Dad's rabbit hunting gun], and Blab took it and left. I was a wreck. I was scared to death Carl was either going to get killed or kill his good friend, Nigger John. Blab was trying to calm me down but said, 'Della, I've got to go. He's [John] liable to kill Carl before I get back!'

I was a wreck a lot of times. He kept me that way half the time!

Mercifully, the antagonism was over by the time Blab returned to Colored Camp.

I can't imagine how long the next few hours were for Mother. Waiting to see if Dad would return, waiting on the wail of an ambulance, the police, waiting, waiting, waiting. She knew many a night like this.

These...what shall we call them – social crises – were frequent and difficult. And hard as they were, the labor skirmishes matched them. Picketing was dangerous business. Mother and Dad both echoed the same sentiment on the matter. Dad said, "I never knowed when I left out of a-mornin' if that would be the last time I'd ever see her again. I never knowed if I'd be alive come evenin', if I'd make it back home."

Mother remarks:

I was always a wreck when Carl would head out on a picket line. I just gave up asking him not to go, I knew it was no use. All day or night, whichever it was for this or that picket, I'd be worried sick. Not knowing was so hard. You just never knew what was going on, if he was okay. It just kept me tore up all the time. I was worried for the rest of them too – Lawrence, and Ed, and Chalk. Well, and I'd have to say others too, our friends. We had so many good friends and they were all miners. I didn't want to see anything happen to any of these men.

As the reader now knows, there was good reason to worry. One of the pickets especially, the one at Crummies Creek, would go horribly wrong. This tragedy led to the single most intense time of emotional stress of the entire era for Mother.

Such was Dad's grief-fueled fury over his brother's murder that his will was set like flint to see to it that he got the man who did it.

I had a .16 gauge Remington automatic shotgun [mentioned in an earlier story], and I went to Coleman's Hardware [Evarts] and got me some .00 buckshot for it. I intended to get that bird, brother! Then I got to thinkin' and changed my mind. I traded my shotgun for a military-issue Colt .45 automatic. If I ever found out who it was that killed my brother, I meant to walk up behind him and shoot him just like he shot Chalk. Then I was going to beat that pistol out over what was left of his head. I had ever' intention of seeing to it that his head ended up lookin' like my brother's did in that morgue!

If you remember from that story, Dad made a promise to his dead brother while clinging to him in the morgue that he would "neither eat, nor drink, nor sleep til [he] got the sonofabitch that done this!" Mother lived with the pressure of this for years. Dad continues:

> I meant to not give him a chance, for he didn't give my brother one! I had my .45 with me all the time for a long while there. I intended to walk up behind him and empty it into his head. Nine shots. For you could put eight in the clip and one in the chamber, you see. I was gonna empty it into his head, just like he did poor ol' Chalk's.
>
> If I couldn't get to that killer and he went to trial, I meant to get in the courthouse with my gun some way or the other. I was gonna get him in that courthouse if that was the only way, buddy. I got out and practiced shootin' at cans and things til I got good with that .45 from a distance. I had it cut and dried for me to get into that courthouse with my pistol somehow. But they didn't bring it to trial, of course. They smothered it out, I reckon.

Mother states:

> He tried every way in the world to find out who did it, every way he could to get any information at all. It's like I told you, honey, he was a wreck there for years over the killing of his brother. He'd go back and forth between sad and mad. He'd go out at night hunting the man, trying to find out who did it. He had me a nervous wreck for years there. He kept me scared to death.

It turns out that Dad spent years looking for a man who was no longer alive. According to George Titler in his illuminating and stirring, *Hell in Harlan*, the alleged shooter was a bulletproof vest–wearing "gun thug" named Bill Lewis. He was gunned down inside the Harlan Courthouse by a young man named William

Deane, just four months after Lewis went on that killing spree in the company store at Crummies Creek. According to Titler, "when Deane was asked why he killed Lewis he said he was trying to win a medal."[74]

The near-constant pressures Mother faced in those days by no means stemmed entirely from Dad's temper and recklessness. Acts born of virtue can cause stress as well.

On a regular basis Dad and several fellow miners met in the office of mine superintendent Vardy McPeek. The purpose of the meeting was specific and the intent serious. This was the meeting of 31's mine rescue team. One of the responsibilities Dad took very seriously was his work as a member of this team. I say responsibility, but he felt it was every bit as much a great privilege. Each mine had its own mine rescue team, which was called to action when a disaster occurred. The team was comprised of regular miners, which is to say that being a part of the team was in addition to, not a replacement for, their regular jobs in the mine. The miners on these teams practiced hard and took their charge seriously. Whenever a disaster occurred at a regional mine, the rescue teams rallied together from all corners to do everything possible to try to save lives. There was (and still is) an annual competition among the teams of all the surrounding mines, to see whose team will be deemed the superior team for the year. In Dad's day, the competition was conducted on the old Harlan High football field. In 1948 the team from Black Mountain's 31 mine won the contest. Each member of the winning team received an engraved silver ring with the white Red Cross symbol mounted on a green and red background on its crown. (Dad gave me his ring many years ago as a keepsake.)

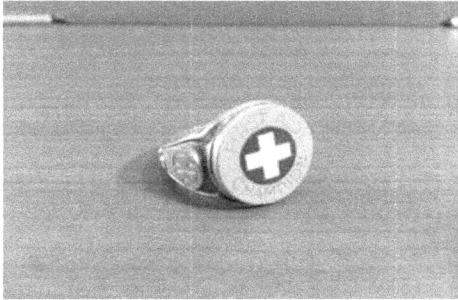

Figure 31. Dad's mine rescue championship ring from the 1948 competition. Note his initials on side.

T. S. Eliot famously describes April as the "cruellest month,"[75] but in Southeastern Kentucky in 1945, December takes that claim.[76] A terrible fate befalls the men of the Belva mine (Kentucky Straight Creek Coal Company in Four Mile, near Pineville), in Bell County. This fate is made even crueler[77] by the timing of the tragedy. It occurs the day after Christmas.

It is about 8:00 a.m., less than an hour after the man trip deposited its load of miners some two miles back in the earth. A violent methane gas[78] or coal dust explosion[79] leads to the dreaded concomitant "thump" felt throughout the camp. Miners and their families know too well what this muffled-yet-sonorous thump means. Smoke and fire spew from the drift mouth so profusely it is impossible to tell whether it is being sucked or shoved. The rush of family members to the mine, surprisingly, is considerably less than typical for a mine disaster. So violent is the explosion, so vigorous the resultant shockwave that it seems families know instinctively that hope, which typically calls families to the tipple, will not be appearing this day.

The mine's own rescue crew jumps feverishly into action. Time is precious. There are more than thirty men trapped inside. The call goes out to area mines, whose rescue crews mobilize and race to the scene. Included in the responders is the 31 mine rescue team from Black Mountain. They will be at the site for four days and nights, as will many of their brother rescuers. Families cry and pray and fret. Neighbors, friends, and fellow mining families from nearby bring food and try to bring comfort. The Salvation Army and the Red Cross show up to do likewise. (Dad was particularly impressed with the ministrations of the Salvation Army during that time – not so much, the Red Cross.)

Mother remarks:

> I was so worried for everybody up there at that mine during those four days. You do some tall praying! That was so sad for them poor people. I was worried for everybody but I knew Carl would try to do anything to get to them poor miners. I was pregnant with Ronnie at the time and I couldn't help but think what I would do with one child already and with another on the way if he got killed in that rescue.

The situation is dire. Most of the miners are near two miles back in the mountain. Rescue teams, gas masks donned, fight monoxide gas, toxic air (black damp[80]), and billowing smoke as they move forward. They extinguish sixteen fires and dig through continuous rubble in knee-deep water just to get to the first major roof collapse. When the nightmare is over, one of the worst mining disasters in Kentucky history will have transpired. (Mrs. Lenore Miller, a Belva widow, says "There's more widows and orphans in this holler than men at work."[81]) Only seven miners will come out alive. Four lifeless, burned bodies will be rescued. The mine becomes a humble and unworthy tomb for twenty men.

Figure 32. Breathing apparatus as used by Dad and other mine rescuers of the day. (Courtesy National Archives. Used by permission.)

As I have said, it's not like life was a continual source of stress and trauma for Mother. She and Dad loved those years of long ago. There were many, many good times – fun times, happy times. Nevertheless, there was a recurrent thread of stress and anxiety woven through life's fabric for Mother then. She knew that pressure throughout all those mining years, yet it never crushed her spirit or deformed her benevolent personality.

During one conversation, Mother and Dad shared a story with me which I will not recount here. It caused me to reflect afresh on just how strong Mother has been through the years. I said, "Mother, it's a wonder you weren't either broken down emotionally or killed by all you've been through!" Mother replied, "That's true, I guess. That's why I say, people don't know what I've gone through." Dad broke in, "That poor little thing's been through a lot, buddy."

He didn't know it but, with those words, Dad summed up the point of this chapter perfectly. As paradoxical as it seems to her gentle and sensitive nature, Mother is an iron-strong woman.

CHAPTER 11

The Good Times

Both Mother and Dad considered the period from about 1940 to the mid-1950s to be their favorite era. The war was over, work was good, and their family had grown again. Their third child, my sister Sandra, was born at the turn of the decade in April, 1950.

Figure 33. My sister, Sandra, in Black Mountain in 1952

The collective sigh of relief over the war's end was felt in the Kentucky hollows as it was everywhere else in this country. The coal business had backed down to a more normal level of production. While work was still plentiful, the feverish wartime demand for coal was past.

One thing demand stayed high for was experiences and the stories which grew out of them. The days of the double shifts were over and the miners had more time at their disposal. Dad and his friend, Blab Davis, used some of that downtime to concoct a day of fun for the men, and profit for themselves. They had decided to have a turkey shoot up in one of the hollows of 31 Camp.

Mother's homemade chili was a solid hit with their group of friends and was served often at the gatherings at their house. (Mother laughingly states, "We had company all the time. Our friends loved to come over so much they kept telling us we ought to open a restaurant. I said, 'Huh! Why, we'd end up with nothing! Carl would get to drinking and having a big time and just set everybody up for free!'")

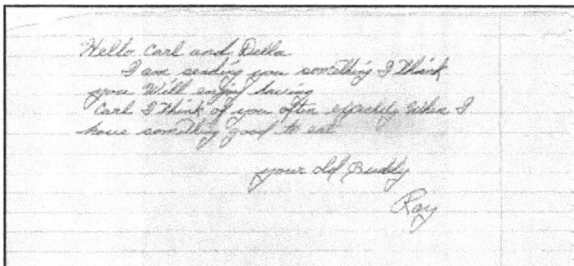

Figure 34. Note from good friend Roy McKamey sent to Mother and Dad much later in life. He was a member of that group of friends which often showed up at their house for those fun times.

Dad and Blab had her make a big pot of chili – "I made it in my dumpling pot," says Mother – to use for the hotdogs they intended to sell at the turkey shoot. They told Mother they would give her the money from the sales of the hotdogs. Dad and Blab planned to sell beer to wash the hotdogs down.

Mother recalls:

Carl and Blab drove to Cumberland to get some cases of beer and to pick up the buns and weenies for the hotdogs. Well, they got everything set up and things got underway with the turkey shoot. They were selling hotdogs as fast as they could make them, and beer to go with them. They were really making the money – at first. But Carl and Blab got to drinking the beer and they got so high on it that they just started telling everybody to help themselves to the beer and hotdogs! After expenses [beer, ice, buns, chili fixings, wieners], they didn't make a dime. They actually lost money! Of course, I never saw a penny of that money I was supposed to get from them hotdogs!

Speaking of Blab Davis, Mother and Dad share an anecdote involving his youngest brother, Frank. Dad says:

Jake and Mrs. Davis lived above us in 31, closer to the tipple. Frank was their baby. Well, when Frank started in the first grade, he did like a lot of the kids and walked the track or the road to the main highway to get to school there up on the hill at 30. Well, when he started on the first day, Frank took down them tracks buddy, and some of 'em noticed he had his baby bottle in one hip pocket of his overalls and a plug of chewin' tobacco in the other one! He was startin' the first grade and I reckon he figured that with his chewin' tobacco and his baby bottle, he was ready to go!

Figure 35. Dad (center) and other members of a booster club "The Rooters" yucking it up at a ball game.

Here is a recollection from Black Mountain in which, for reasons that will become obvious, the names have been changed. Dad had a friend, Cliff, who was a bit "slow," as they say. Cliff's wife, Frieda, was a most attractive woman with a robust amorous appetite. More plainly, Frieda liked men. A lot.

We was a-sittin' and eatin' lunch in the mines and Cliff come out with this story. 'Boy, o' Frieder [he pronounced her name as though it ended in "r"] ain't afraid of nothin'. Some feller come to the

208

door last night and he said somethin' that must have made Frieder mad for she lit out after him and run him til way up in the night. It was near mornin' when she come back in!

Dad says you have never in your life seen a group of men working harder to contain their laughter. One or two actually had to walk away for a bit! He goes on:

I remember another one of Cliff's stories too. Cliff had gone home early from work one day for some reason or another. It was a-rainin' that day. When he got home, he caught Frieda by surprise. She wasn't expectin' him that time of day, buddy! Poor ol' Cliff said, 'I walked in the bedroom and they was some man in there in the bed with Frieder and they was just a-carryin' on. That made me mad. Ol' Cliff got him though. Ol' Cliff got him good. I frowed ["throwed"] his ol' hat out in the rain!'

I mentioned that the first of the two "Cliff" stories above occurred as the miners were on their lunch break. Lunchtime practical joking seems to have been a regular part of the Black Mountain miner's life. Miners carried their lunches in either a "lunch kit" or a "lunch bucket." The kit is the container with the thermos in the lid when you open it. The bucket is an older device, with stacking sections. Miners didn't carry their lunches in paper bags, the mine rats would have it eaten by lunchtime. Dad remarks, "Some of them rats in the mine had been there so long they had service stripes. And some of 'em was so big you could harness 'em and pull out a car of coal!"

Here's one of Dad's lunchtime stories:

I remember I couldn't wait til lunch for I was a-gettin' hungry and Della always packed me a good lunch, buddy. They'd be a couple of sandwiches, fruit, and a cake or some other sweet. When I got my lunch kit I knowed somethin' was wrong. It was too light, you see. Somebody had cut my lunch. [Their expression for it.] Somebody got my lunch and eat ever' bit of it, buddy! I didn't know who, but somebody had eat ever' last bit of it.

Well, nobody said nothin', and I didn't either. Somebody had got me good! At quittin' time Howard – Howard Kidd – and Cecil Stafford come up to me and said, 'Carl, see if Della will add another sandwich or two tomorrow. Them was good!' One of 'em said, 'Man, Della shore packs a good lunch! And see if she'll add another cake or two, that wouldn't be bad!' They was just a-laughin' up a storm!

I waited a few days and then I got 'em, buddy. I eat Cecil's first. I eat everything he had! I remember he had an apple. I eat it and started to put the core back in his bucket and I thanks 'Nope, I'll just eat that too!' And I did. I eat core and all! His wife had put him some milk in the bottom and I even drunk his milk too. I put water in it then, where the milk was.

At dinnertime [lunch], Cecil saw he didn't have nothin at all in there but some water. He just looked up and said, 'Well, if we was out of milk I wish the ol' lady had let me know.' He knowed somethin' was up, you see. He was just goin' along with it.

I eat Howard Kidd's next. I don't remember what he had but I know I eat ever bit of it, buddy! At dinner, ol' Howard didn't even open his bucket when he picked it up. He just shook his head and laughed.

The third one that had been in on it was Zes Bolen. Zes had some bacon and about three biscuits and some oatmeal. I eat ever bit of his too!

At dinnertime I got my lunch kit out and said, 'Whew, I'm shore glad it's dinnertime. I can't wait to eat; I'm starved to death!' I wasn't of course. I was as full as a tick, buddy, for I'd done eat three lunches! I opened my lunch kit and was about to start eatin'. Zes said, 'I told you! I told you Carl Rue' – he always said both my names, but he couldn't pronounce 'Ruth' – he said 'I told you Carl Rue would get even with us. I told you he'd get us!'

They all had a good laugh, and then Dad gave them his lunch to share among themselves.

Black Mountain had a man renowned for his stories, practical jokes, and pranks. His name was Oscar Lay, but everybody knew him as "Did" Lay. Laughingly, Dad says, "Buddy, everybody knowed nobody was in Did Lay's league when it come to tellin' 'em'!" He didn't mean malicious lying, just the way Did Lay was always telling yarns. Among my favorite are these:

Did Lay said he went up in the mountains one time and he set down under a chinkapin [oak] for a bit to rest for a spell from the climb. He said all of a sudden he heard a racket and a commotion, and a rattler – a rattlesnake – was a-comin' right at him. He said that rattler reared up and struck right at his face. Did moved just in time and that rattler struck the oak he was a-sittin' against.

Well, Did said all of a sudden that tree went to swellin' and before it was done, it was three times its size. Did said he cut that tree down, milled the lumber, and built him a five room house out of it!

That would have stretched the imaginative powers of most men to their limit. But not Did Lay! Dad continues:

Did said Bess, his wife, was a-paintin' their new house, which Did had built with the swollen wood from that oak. She had a bottle of turpentine there to thin the paint. Well, Bess accidentally knocked that bottle of turpentine over and when it hit the wood, it commenced to take the swellin' from the snakebite out-a that wood, buddy!

Did said that by the time it finished a-shrinkin', he could pick that house up in his hands. He said he just took it and nailed it to a tree for sparrows to use!

Did Lay's pranks rivaled his stories. For example:

Did had run into a couple of fellers he knowed down at the store and asked 'em if they wanted to make a little money. He said he had a couple hogs that needed butcherin' and that he didn't have the time to tend to it. He said if they'd cut the hogs up for him, he'd pay 'em.

Well, they jumped at that, buddy! Did told 'em to go on down to the house and go over by the creek and get their fire a-goin'. He said, 'Get your water boilin' and get ready but wait an hour or so to go to the house. Bess won't be up that early and I don't want you to wake her.'

Well, they did as they was told. They got their fire ready and got their water a-boilin'. They waited a bit and then they went and knocked on the door. One of 'em said to Bess, 'We're here to kill them hogs for you. Did sent us.'

Bess said, 'Hogs?! Lord have mercy, we ain't got no hogs!'

That was Did Lay!

July was vacation time for the miners. The mines would shut down for the first week of the month, so the men could be off for the Fourth, and folk would head off for some well-earned rest and recreation. For Mother and Dad and friends, that usually meant camping and fishing at Deep Cove Lodge in Knoxville, Tennessee. (It's funny how life unwinds. My family and I now live about ten minutes away from where Deep Cove Lodge was located.)

The men spent each and every day of vacation fishing hard and running trotlines and enjoying the camaraderie that meant so much to them. In preparation for setting out trotlines, the guys would seine minnows for bait. Dad remembers:

Me and Ansil King and his little boy – he was about 10, I reckon – was seining near the fresh spring there up near Pineville, where people stop to get water. We was up in a small cove there in the backwater. We caught this little ol' bass minnow time and again, and we'd throw it back. You can't bait with that, you see, for it's a game fish. It's illegal. Well, sure enough, that thing showed up in our net again and Ansil was gettin' tired of foolin' with it. He said, 'If we catch that thing one more time, I'm fixin' it good!' Well, shore enough we did. Ansil just picked that thing up and swollered it down, buddy! [Dad starts laughing.] That shocked his little boy, when Ansil done that. He looked at me right bug-eyed like and said, 'Did you see that! That damn fool swollered that thing!' [Mountain sushi.]

While on vacation, the wives spent the day lounging in the sun, having lunch together at the very good Deep Cove restaurant which overlooked the lake, and watching the hive of activity in motion lakeside. It is funny to think of Mother on a trip like this for vacation. She is no fan of boat rides, doesn't fish, has never tasted fish of any kind, and, in fact, eats no seafood whatsoever. (Although she loves hushpuppies!) Oh yeah, and she can't swim!

Learning that Deep Cove had a fine dance floor solved the riddle for me. In the evening there was plenty of dancing and many good memories built. Mother recalls that a number of students from the University of Tennessee (just a short drive away from Deep Cove) came down in the evening for the music and dancing. Those evenings were such great fun, as Mother recalls.

I discovered one surprising bit of information about Mother as she, Dad, and I talked one day about their vacations at Deep Cove. She said the only time she ever wore pedal pushers or slacks was when they were on vacation. Like most of the married camp women, she wore dresses or skirts. Mother says she didn't begin to wear slacks regularly until we moved to Knoxville, in 1965. This is peculiar to me because, except for church, weddings, or other special occasions, I can't recall her wearing anything but slacks (or shorts, in her earlier years).

I mentioned that my maternal grandmother, "Mom," lived with us for all but the first year of so of their marriage. While Mother and Dad were on vacation, my siblings were home with Mom, no doubt having a vacation of their own with her. Mom saw to it that they had fun that week, and each of them has a cache of priceless memories to prove it.

One of the activities Mom arranged with my siblings was to take them on "cookouts." In the evening, after dinner, she would take them up past the tipple in 31 and they would have a time. Mom would take a skillet and a few potatoes and she would build a cook fire and fry the potatoes for them. As everyone had already eaten dinner, this was just part of the role play of the cookout. The mine had its sand piles in that same area and after eating, the kids would play in the sand piles and in the shuttle cars at the foot of the tracks. When it was time to go, it was just a short walk back up the tracks to home.

———————————

Dad shares a tale with me that sounds just like the script of a western. As I wrote that last sentence, it immediately occurred to me that half the stories in this book read like they are straight out of old Dodge City. For example:

Shelby Howard run a beer joint. [Mother thinks it was in Evarts.] Some fellers there were kindly drunk and one of 'em got into it with Shelby. Well, Shelby run the guy off and as he was a-leavin' he turned around at Shelby and said, 'I'll be back!' That man was called Hayslinger. I don't know if that was his name or a nickname, but he was called Hayslinger.

They was a pool room joinin' the beer joint and me and a few other guys was in there shootin' craps on the back pool table. There was just a doorway between the two rooms. [A good many of the miners liked to shoot pool there. My uncle, Sine, who was an excellent pool player, liked to play there.]

Well, Shelby had walked in there where we was shootin' craps, in the pool room part, and was a-watchin' us. Dreckly [directly] that feller he run off come back and he had a .410 gauge shotgun. He stood in that partition between the two rooms and commenced to unload at Shelby with that shotgun, buddy!

Well, Shelby's down here next to where we was shootin' craps on the pool table. He was hunkered down under that pool table a-shootin' up over the top of it with his pistol. Or a-tryin' to! That .38 of his went to snappin' but wouldn't fire!

When them two went to shootin' all of 'em that was in the crap game with me run out. I laughed and said, 'Well, I guess I'm the house man! I just scooted up the money and stuck it in my pocket!'

As you can probably imagine, a good many of Dad's stories were head shakers to me, but I was absolutely gobsmacked by this one! I think you will see why as you read on.

"Wait, Dad. Are you telling me that two guys are having a shootout, and a man with a shotgun is firing in your direction at another man, who is hunched behind a pool table right beside the one you're standing at?"

"Yeah."

"Weren't you afraid you'd get hit in the crossfire?"

"No."

216

"Why?!"

"He wasn't a-shootin' at me."

Ooookay.

I remember having two thoughts at that moment. One, who in the world thinks like that in such a situation! Two, what on earth has kept this man alive! Dad continues the story:

> Shelby's .38 wouldn't fire a lick! It just kept a-snappin'. [Dad is laughing heartily as he recalls this story. In fact, this is the hardest he laughed throughout this entire journey.] He kept raisin' his arm over that pool table and pullin' the trigger but his pistol just wouldn't shoot. He was just a-jabberin' that whole time and a-cussin' at his gun! Hayslinger was hunkered down by the jukebox at that partition between the rooms a-shootin'.
>
> Well, one of his shots caught Shelby. It didn't catch him clean; it wasn't a kill shot or nothin'. Shelby looked over at me and said, 'Lord, I'm dying Carl!' [Dad's laughing so hard telling this he literally has tears.]
>
> I said 'Newwwww [Noooo], you ain't dyin' Shelby.' I said, 'A man goin' on like you can't be dyin'!'
>
> When Hayslinger saw that Shelby was hit, he took off out of the building. I finally got Shelby quietened down somewhat and called the ambulance. I rode with him to try to keep him calm til we got him up the hill there to the Black Mountain Hospital.

The final chapter of this story is so very telling. In fact, it shows again the mountain mindset so clearly:

Shelby's dad, Tom, come back to where we was, in the back of the hospital there where they had Shelby. He had got word and had got to the hospital by this time, you see. I'll never forget this. Tom walked in pointin' his finger at Shelby the whole way and saying, 'Let that be a lesson to you, buddy. When he told you he'd be back, why wasn't you ready for him? Why'd you ever let him get back in there?!' I'll never forget that.

Not, "Are you hurt bad, son?" Not, "What has the doctor said?" None of that. Tom Howard's burning question to his son was "Why were you so foolish as to let that man get the drop on you?!"

Harlan County back then was the wettest dry county[82] you'll ever see. There were plenty of sources for bootlegged liquor, but many preferred to make their own. Some of the Italian immigrants, like Dad's friend in Punkin Center, Andy Companite, made wine. Others, including Dad, occasionally made home brew (beer). Some, of course, made moonshine whiskey.[83] One of Dad's shining friends used to boldly walk down Main Street in Evarts with a gallon jug of his finest. "Buddy, they're gonna catch you with that one of these days and you'll be up the creek," says Dad. His friend replies, "Nah, they'll just think it's a jug of kerosene for an oil lamp."

Every so often, agents of the Internal Revenue Service – revenuers – would make a run on the hills of Black Mountain in search of moonshine stills. The shiners generally knew when they were on the way because they would get word from fellow shiners in nearby locations. Dad shares the following:

--- --- was a well-known moonshiner and the revenuers was a-tryin' to catch him and tryin' to find his still. This was in the spring, near Easter time.

Well, he had a young girl and them revenuers thought they could butter her up and get what they was lookin' for out of her. They told her, 'You tell us where your daddy's still is and we'll buy you a nice Easter outfit.' They said, 'All you have to do is take us to his still and we'll give you the money for that outfit.'

---'s girl said, 'Well, give me the money now.' They said, 'No. We'll give it to you when we get back from the still.' She said, 'Huh-uh. Give it to me now. 'Cause if you go up in that mountain you ain't comin' back!'

What follows is my favorite moonshine whiskey story of all those I ever heard Dad tell. I think. I have to admit that I am pretty fond of the previous one as well! This story takes place as Dad runs into a 'shine-selling friend of his coming down the railroad tracks one day.

Dad: Ed, how's your business a-doin'?

Ed: Man, it's goin' to town. Carl, I'm sellin' it as fast as I can make it, buddy.

Dad: How much you sellin' it for?

Ed: Fifty cents a pint.

Dad: [After calculating approximately how much it would cost to make per pint.] You can't be making no money, buddy!

Ed: No Carl, I ain't. But I've got a hell of a lot of business! [cliff ape!]

While not a moonshine story per se, this would be an appropriate place to share the account of a wake Dad attended in Black Mountain. (Regrettably, Dad could not remember the name of the deceased.) An Irish miner had died and Dad went to the wake at the boarding house where he had lived, to pay his respects. The Irish are well known for their ability to throw a good going-away party for their deceased, and this one was no exception. Dad says:

I went up to the casket and, buddy, they wasn't nobody in it! And I mean, they wasn't no *body* in it! The room was full of people but they wasn't no corpse in the casket! I didn't know what to make of that and didn't know what to do. I moved away from the coffin and was lookin' around the room. Then I seen him. Buddy, they had that corpse a-standin' up in the corner! They had a derby hat on his head and a drink in his hand! I never will forget that. That was too much for me. I got outta there, buddy!

We are Irish on the Ruth side of our family (County Kilkenny), but that experience was too much even for a fellow Irishman like Dad! I always got a good laugh out of hearing him tell the story of that wake.

As with all things, the good times would not last forever. The '40s would give way to the '50s and the '50s would eventually bring an end to significant mining in Black Mountain.

On October 5, 1956, Mother would give birth to their last child – yours truly. (I was born 13 days after Dad's mother, Grandma Ruth, passed away.) By this time the UMWA had funded the building of the Harlan Appalachian Regional Hospital. To the miners it was simply, the Miners' Hospital.

Figure 36. L to R: Dad, Uncle Ed, Uncle Ervin, unknown man, Uncle
Lawrence at the burial of Grandma Ruth.

As previously noted, Mother preferred having her
children at home because she preferred the privacy of
that approach. In her word she was so "backward" she
didn't want to deliver in the hospital. "You know me, I
used to be so backward. I'd rather have my babies at the
house." I smiled at her and said, "Used to be?" She
chuckled and replied, "Yeah, used to be."

In 1956, law no longer allowed this option. So I,
unlike my three siblings, was born in the hospital.

By that same year, it was becoming increasingly clear
that the handwriting was on the wall for Black
Mountain mining. (In 1960 Harlan County would mine
less coal than it had in 50 years.) In the spring of 1958,

the mine closed. I inquired as to the cause of this and Dad replies:

It was tearing up the equipment, honey. The coal had got down so low [short seams] that it was tearin' up the shuttle cars and such. It got to where they didn't think the profit per ton was big enough to pay union scale to mine it. They just went down in Western Kentucky where they had them big dippers and stripped it [strip mining].

I kept tellin' them fellers [co-miners] that it was gonna close and they didn't believe it. I said, 'Yeah! Yeah it is too!' I said, 'Peabody [Peabody Coal Co., Peoria, Illinois – parent company of the Black Mountain mines] ain't up here to go in the hole, just to keep us a place to work!' I said, 'Oh yeah, it's gonna close!'

Jim Douglas [company official] told me they had thirty-five years of work there still, but it was just costin' 'em too much to mine it. I knowed we was in trouble when they went to payin' by the shift. [Near the end, even cash advances were given in currency and not in scrip.] A machine man and the loader, the man that loaded the coal, was the highest paid men on the job, for they was the most dangerous jobs, you see. When that machine is a-cuttin' coal and the loader's runnin', they's so much racket you can't hear if the top's a-workin' [ceiling shifting] or hear the timbers crack. That's a spooky sound, man! It's dangerous, buddy. But these fellers, the machine man and his helper and the loader man got to gettin' paid by the shift. I knowed we was shuttin' down when the company went to doin' this.

This was the end of an era.

Figure 37. Timbers buckling under an oppressive roof. (Courtesy Dave Johnson. Used by permission.)

It is easy to overlook how significant this period of time is, both historically and socioeconomically as far as Harlan County and other mining-dependent areas are concerned. How different would the coal business of Southern Appalachia look today had the struggles to organize mining labor not taken place all those years ago – struggles that cost those men and families involved dearly? Would the operators have evolved into altruistic men who, seeing a shining light that showed them the errors of their ways, decided to share the power and wealth with the workers who enriched them? (He says, with tongue firmly planted in cheek.) I heartily doubt that. Would the government have finally stepped in to correct the imbalances? Not likely, unless such a hue and cry arose from the citizenry over the plight of miners that the politicians' fear of losing votes overrode their fear of losing the payoffs (and maybe their lives) from the coal barons. As one Harlan County politician put it: "The coal operators have a hell of a lot of influence in the elections. If they are not for you, it is too bad..."[84]

We don't know what *might* have happened over time. We only know what *did* happen because workers became sufficiently angry and fed up with so unjust a system that they did something about it.

Socioeconomically, Harlan County and similar rural mining regions are still paying a high and hard cost for the fact that the coal barons back then had a clinched grip around the necks of the local governments and the economies of those regions – a grip that intentionally prevented other businesses and industries from coming in. This power grab by a single, monopolistic entity prevented free-market enterprise. When that controlling monopoly pulled out, they left nothing but a hole.[85]

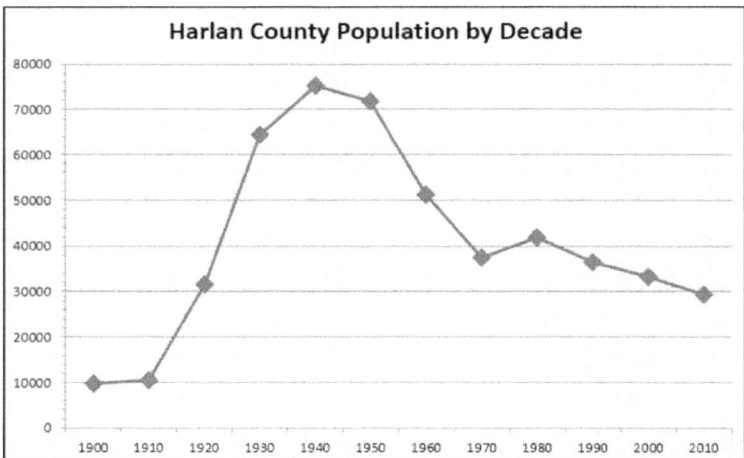

Figure 38. Note the continual and ongoing decline following the end of the coal boom years.

Having been told that the mine closed in '58, and knowing that we didn't move to Harlan until 1959, I asked Dad what he did in the intervening time. Dad answers:

> Well, me and Sine went to Cincinnati to try and get work, didn't we honey? (Mother confirms, 'Yeah. Yeah you did. You and Sine.') But we couldn't find no work. Well, it wasn't long til Christmas, and me and Sine went to Louisville to try to find some work before Christmas. We stayed across the river in Jeffersonville, Indiana, with my brother Ervin and his family.
>
> Me and Sine worked in a department store, wrappin' Christmas packages and I worked a second job of a night at a gas station there. We was workin' to get money for Christmas. We couldn't find permanent work, so we come back home right before Christmas.

Mother adds, "Even though the mine closed, we had a great Christmas that year, just like we always did."

This had to be so hard on Dad and Sine. Two career miners, the job they so loved behind them now, in a big city, a city unknown to either of them, wrapping Christmas presents to earn money. It demonstrates how seriously they took their responsibilities to provide for their families. I'll always admire, respect, and appreciate both of them for this.

> I remember that when we got back home Earl Carlisle [a mine official], said he'd sell me that house we lived in there in Black Mountain. I said, 'Lord, I don't need that house, buddy. There ain't

no work here. I've got a family to keep up. I've got
to get out of here and get work!'

Get out of Black Mountain and find work, he did.
Dad's brother Ed, a former superintendent at Black
Mountain, knowing that mine was about to play out,
took a superintendent's job at the Hyden mine. As soon
as possible, he hired Dad.

Mother states that we stayed in Black Mountain until
Dad could find us a house. He had gone ahead to
Harlan and was staying with Uncle Ed and his family on
Poplar Street.

On October 9, 1959, four days after my third
birthday, we moved to 201 Sycamore Street in Harlan.
My earliest memories trace to this address. Being so
young when we left there, I have no personal memories
whatsoever associated with Black Mountain.

PART THREE

BLACK MOUNTAIN
TO HARLAN

CHAPTER 12

Mining Takes Its Toll

Old-school mining was back-breaking labor. Ever see a picture of a miner lying on his side, propped up on the inverted bucket of his shovel, picking coal from a seam because the roof was so low he couldn't get on his knees? A cubic yard of coal weighs just over one ton. That's some hard picking and shoveling. The work was as dangerous as it was strenuous.

Figure 39. Setting timbers in 28-inch coal. (Courtesy Dave Johnson. Used by permission.)

The major repercussions to Dad's body from a career in mining are numerous. Two of these, I've shared with you already – the loss of most of his left thumb and the left side of his hand, including his little finger. These injuries left him with just three fingers on his left hand. (During WWII, Dad, ever the humorist, would hold those three fingers up and say, "Them are the big three!" History buffs will remember this to be the tag given to the Allied leaders: Churchill, Roosevelt, and Stalin.)

Like the two before it, the third of Dad's major mining injuries occurred while mining at Black Mountain. The year is 1950, and summer is fading to fall. Dad explains:

> I was a-drillin' the face at the time. Drillin' to shoot [dynamite]. We had these powerful drills with augers on 'em, you see, and we'd drill holes in the face to put the dynamite in, to blast the face of the coal. That's called shootin' the coal. Well, I was drillin' the face and that bit caught rock, buddy. That thing jerked me so hard when it caught that I thought it had broke my back. I was in such pain I liked to passed out. I remember I couldn't hardly move.

That violent jerk resulted in a slipped disc. Dad was taken to the Black Mountain Hospital for examination, and spent several days in traction there. His doctor concluded that surgery was needed. Dad's friend and boss, K. P. Floyd, came to visit him in the hospital. Dad recalls, K. P. said, "Carl, whatever you do don't let them operate on your back in this hospital. You get out of here and get to Knoxville, or somewhere else. Don't you dare let them do it here." Mother adds, "The nurses in the Black Mountain Hospital at that time were great but the doctors weren't as good, at least not good enough to want them to do back surgery on you."

Figure 40. Drilling the face as Dad was doing when injured. (Courtesy British Coal Corporation. Used by permission.)

Dad followed Mr. Floyd's advice and was transferred to the Baptist Hospital, in Knoxville. He was thirty-four years old and mining had now cost him a third significant physical injury.

This latest affliction came at a most inopportune time, for Mother had not long since given birth to my sister Sandra. Born earlier that same year, she was still in arms. This was just one of the many, many times our family was blessed to have Mom in-house. She stayed in Black Mountain and tended to Pat and Ronnie while Mother brought Sandra with her to Knoxville. Aunt Goldie and my Uncle T. W. lived in Knoxville, and Mother stayed with them so she could be near Dad.

231

When Mother would go to the hospital to be with Dad, Aunt Goldie would tend to Sandra for her.

Mother recalls Dad's words to her as he was being rolled into surgery. True to his ways he looked up at her, waved, smiled, and said, "Toodle-oo. If I don't see you again, plant your taters where you did last year!" That took a bit of the edge off the moment for Mother. She just shook her head at Dad and laughed.

The fourth major physical blow to come at Dad from mining differed from the previous three in a distinct way. This one did not occur on a given day, at a given time. In the mid-1970s, Dad was diagnosed with that most dreaded of all mining consequences: the miner's cough – pneumoconiosis – black lung. It is the result of many years of breathing coal dust in the mines, dust which the human lung was never designed to house. Dad mined for twenty-eight years. That's a lot of coal dust.

Figure 41. Left is healthy lung tissue, right is lung tissue of a miner who died from black lung. (Courtesy National Archives. Used by permission.)

For the last quarter of his life, Dad struggled with shortness of breath and diminished stamina, the result of black lung. Not infrequently he would awake at night due to difficulty breathing ("smotherin'"). With black lung, breathing is often harder lying down. So he would sit up during those "spells" and like his father before him, sleep in a chair. His nebulizer was never far away.

Cataloging the physical injuries does not take into account the concomitant psychological consequences. Though he made the very best of it, and I never once heard him complain about it, losing portions of one's hand creates a staring point. The heartiest of spirits would have to be a little self-conscious of this.   In addition, the back injury meant that Dad could not work at all for a while, and then only light duty for a long span after that. This was hard on a pull-your-load guy like Dad. He was relieved when he could return again to his normal work duties.

Difficult as they were, each of these matters paled in comparison, psychologically, to the toll taken by the murder of his brother and best friend, Chalk. Dad never got over that. I don't mean by that he never forgot it – of course he didn't. I mean, he never got over it. "I cry every Memorial Day a-thinkin' about Chalk. I can't help it. I never will get over that, I reckon." Dad told me this fifty-five years after Chalk's death.

Dad would know one final blow of suffering and heartbreak from mining. This one too would involve family and would leave a great scar. It would be another of those things that would accompany Dad to his grave.

Coal-yard Facts

Over 100,000 coal miners were killed in mining accidents in the twentieth century. More than 3,200 of those were in 1907 alone. On Dec 6 of that year, an explosion at the Fairmont Coal Company mine in Monongah, West Virginia, took the lives of 362 men and boys. This is still the worst mining disaster in American history.

CHAPTER 13

A Final Calamity

As noted in Chapter 11, after the Black Mountain Mine closed in 1958, Dad obtained work with his brother, Ed. Uncle Ed, as stated, was now a superintendent at the Hyden mine. To his delight, Dad was once again mining.

We lived just a few blocks away from Uncle Ed, in Harlan – he and his family on Poplar Street, we on Sycamore. This made it easy for Dad and Uncle Ed to commute to Hyden together. Though not as close as he and Chalk, Dad loved his brother Ed dearly. "Ed was a good man, a good Christian," says Dad. He goes on to share the story of an ill-fated day:

We had to get up early and leave way before daylight to get to work on time. We'd go through Harlan and across the old Baxter Bridge and up Baxter Road, and then turn left to go across Pine Mountain. That's how we'd go to Hyden.

Well, it was December, 1959, and me and Ed was headed to work. It had snowed the night before and I remember, man it was sooo cold early that mornin'. Ed had a ragtop Jeep and it was even cold in that Jeep, even with the heat on. I was a-drivin'. Ed always switched seats when he got to the house to pick me up.

Well, we was goin' over Pine Mountain and it was treacherous. We was goin' real slow because we was lookin' for black ice, you see. We could see ice, regular ice, on the side of the road but we wasn't concerned about that. It's that black ice on the road, that ice you can't see til you're on it, that we was afraid of. Well, we come up on a curve and I seen it, that black ice. We wasn't goin' fast. I knowed the road, knowed that curve was there, and we had slowed for it. That ice had an ol' gray spooky look. I didn't get excited or nothin' when I seen it. I had the wheel set to make that curve.

Well, when I hit that black ice, it must have been the position of the steering wheel see, a-goin' around that curve, it just put me in a skid. [Mother interjects, "He said he did everything he'd ever heard of to try to correct it."] We was slidin' so slow a man could have took his hands and stopped our skid. If a guardrail had been there we wouldn't have done nothin' more than just bump it and stop. We was goin' that slow.

But as fate, or bad luck, or blind random probability, or whatever would have it, there was no guardrail there that dark, icy morning.

We spun around real slow a time or two on the road there. It was so slow it felt like we was in slow motion. When I seen we was a-goin' over the cliff, I told Ed to duck down. I got down as low as

I could but couldn't get too low, for the steering wheel blocked me.

I remember we rolled over three times, a-tumblin' down that cliff. Ever' time it'd roll it'd throw me back against the ragtop of that Jeep. They was big ol' rocks on that cliff side, where they had blasted for the road and we was a-tumblin' over them. On one of them flips we slammed one of them rocks so hard that the jolt caused me to bite my tongue nearly in two.

I remember our last flip. We ended up in the icy river at the bottom of the gorge. Our Jeep landed in the water on the driver's side. I remember for I was jammed up against the driver's side of the jeep. The water was ten feet deep and it was freezin' cold.

I knowed Ed wasn't in the Jeep with me. I tried to feel for him and I remember trying to shout his name. I couldn't shout for I was under water. I knowed he wasn't in the Jeep but I didn't know if it had slung him out or what.

I interrupted to ask Dad if at any point while the vehicle was tumbling over the cliff, he had been knocked unconscious.

No, I was just addled like, honey. Kindly [kind of] dazed. I don't remember gettin' out of that Jeep, or gettin' out of that deep water. If I'd had a belt on like they require today, I'd a-drowned. When I come up [to the surface of the river] I hollered and hollered for Ed the best I could, but he never answered. With my tongue bit nearly off I couldn't say his name right, but I was calling out the best I could. I couldn't see a thing for it was still dark, you see. The sun was nowhere near comin' up.

I remember gettin' myself to the bank. I could hardly do it, but I finally got there. I seen lights up on Pine Mountain and I thanks, 'Well, if I can climb up there, get up there to the road somehow, I can get help.' I liked to never got up there. And I kept callin' to Ed the whole time, as best as I could. I got to the road and a milk truck passed – a Chappell's Dairy milk truck from Harlan. I didn't get there in time to stop him. Then another feller was comin' in a truck and I got him waved down.

I asked him to call the ambulance and a wrecker, for I said, 'My brother, I don't know whether he's killed but he's either killed or hurt or knocked out for I've called and called but...' [Dad chokes up here. We pause a few minutes to let him compose himself.]

I was froze. My feet and even my clothes froze on me while I was a-talkin' to that man. You've heard of froze stiff? Well, my britches legs was froze stiff. They was even froze to the ground. I had to jerk my legs to break them loose.

A couple more vehicles had got there by then and some of 'em got me in a car and took me down to some feller's house down the road a little ways. I remember standin' by the stove there in his house til the bus come by. They stopped the bus and I got on it and rode it to Harlan. When I got to the bus station there in Harlan, I got me a taxi then to take me on home. I wasn't in no shape to walk home.

Mother met Dad at the door and when she saw him she was horrified. He was beat to pieces and a bloody mess. She called a taxi and they went straight to the hospital. Aside from more cuts and bruises than one could count, Dad had bitten his tongue almost completely in half and he had broken both collarbones. Between his multiple injuries and his wrenching panic over his brother Ed, I can't imagine what that long bus ride back to Harlan must have been like.

Uncle Ed was dead. On the last tumble of the Jeep, he had either been killed by the rocks or crushed by the vehicle. Although he was found partially in the water, he had not drowned. The autopsy revealed there was no water in the lungs.

Later that morning, a wife and six children would hear the awful news that a husband, a father, would not be coming home. The only consolation to be found had come from the coroner, who assured the family that, like Uncle Chalk before him, Uncle Ed had died suddenly. It wasn't much, but it was something.

Dad wasn't told of Uncle Ed's death for about a week, three or four days after the funeral. He was still in the hospital recovering, and the doctors were keeping him heavily medicated. This was, of course, due to the injuries he had sustained and the pain he was in. Another reason was to keep Dad impervious to his brother's death. They were concerned about the emotional effect the news would have on him, in his condition. Moreover, Mother made it clear to his doctor that it would be impossible to keep him from leaving the hospital to attend the funeral, if he knew about it. He was in no state to do that.

Uncle Ed is buried in Rest Haven Cemetery, in Harlan. On a recent trip to Harlan, Mother and I went to his grave to pay our respects. His stone reads:

Edward L. Ruth
1910 - 1959
A Faithful Servant At Rest In Peace

On each side of the headstone is a concrete vase. Each vase contains a new bouquet of beautiful forget-me-not flowers. I say a silent prayer for comfort for the loved one who put them there.

Figure 42. Uncle Ed's grave. Rest Haven Cemetery, Harlan.

CHAPTER 14

The End of Mining

This final tragedy brought an end to mining once and for all. The labor that Dad so loved, the work that he identified himself with, was gone forever. For the first time in his regularly employed life, a life which began when he was fifteen, Dad was not a miner.

With time, Dad's wounds from the accident healed – the physical ones, anyway. Dad would soon get another job. It was the first of his occupations I remember. He went to work as a deliveryman for Wardrup's Meat Packing Company in Harlan. It is ironic that I sit here writing a book about Dad as a coal miner. As I said in the Preface, I never knew Dad the miner. Also, for the first time in this writing, I am not relying on the memories of others for content.

But the story, in essence, is over. This book is *Memory of a Miner*. Dad, as I have said, would go on to have several more occupations in his life. He would bring his best and give his best to each of them. That's the only ethic he knew. But none who knew Dad would say that he *was* any of those things. What Dad *was*, was a miner. His favorite memories were mining memories. His favorite stories were mining stories. His favorite people were miners.

I've often wondered what it was like for Dad making his deliveries while working at Wardrup's. His routes took him by sites barbed with memories. He drove by former scenes of hostile pickets. He crossed the bell crossing, epicenter of the Battle of Evarts. He routinely went past Coxton. He delivered in Crummies Creek, where Chalk was killed, and in Harlan, where he first saw him in the morgue. He had to traverse Pine Mountain, site of that awful wreck that claimed another brother. I sit and I wonder what those trips were like for him, alone in that panel van.

I remember many great times in Harlan. It's funny, the memories that choose to anchor themselves in your mind from childhood. I remember my seventh birthday, when Mother took me to Mike's Drive-in. I had a "Mike's Special," which was doubly special to me as a youngster then because my name is Mike. Mike's Special was a hamburger with all the trimmings, with an olive toothpicked through the top of the bun and an order of onion rings or French fries. I had onion rings that day, and a strawberry milkshake.

Another memory I still carry with me involves a small, family-owned business just a couple of blocks from where we lived – Faulkner's Grocery. Faulkner's sat on the left just across the old bridge (now gone) from Harlan as you entered the area known as Fairview. Though a grocer, Mr. Faulkner also made and sold hotdogs – the finest in all the world to my mind, both then and now. His famous chili recipe, so closely guarded, was given to Mother later on. She has since passed it down to her children. I make hotdogs frequently (just this past weekend, in fact), using Mr. Faulkner's wonderful chili recipe. When I do, I think of walking up Sycamore, turning left onto May Street and crossing over to Mr. Faulkner's Grocery for one of his mouth-watering hotdogs.

Sycamore Street was a dead end and was therefore safe for play. It was also a good place, because there was no through traffic, to have what today would be called a block party. We had a number of them while we lived in Harlan, and they were great fun.

A real plus was the fact that not long after we moved to Harlan, Sine, Dollie and their sons Bill and Larry, my cousins, moved to Harlan as well. Sine, too, lost his job when the mine closed and had to find other work. Their relocation delighted all of us, but none as much as Mother. Her best friend, her sister Dollie, not only lived in Harlan now, but virtually right across the street. They, too, now lived on Sycamore. It was great!

Dad built a brick barbecue pit in our yard, which was well used during the block parties. The thing was amazing to me. It had raised arms on each side of the grill area, ideal for setting platters, a big pot of sauce for basting, and cooking implements on while preparing the meats. The screen of the grill was a piece of shaker screen from the Black Mountain tipple. I can still recall how sizeable the grilling area was. It was big enough to easily handle the cooking for the parties and certainly enough to accommodate family cookouts (which always included several family friends). Dad had built this pit with a chimney included in its design. The chimney was about four feet high and was constructed with an internal flu. The chimney would actually draw the smoke off the coals up and out.

I loved to stay close by Dad when he barbecued. As a child, I was fascinated by the ritual. Working for Wardrup's meant there was a plethora of meats for the feast. Dad cooked ribs and chicken and pork chops and burgers and hot dogs and copious amounts of each. I can hear Dad's words still: "To cook barbecue right, you just about have to starve yourself to death. You have to be patient, cook it slow, then sauce it in rounds so the sauce bakes in. You have to let that sauce bake in and build a good coatin'."

Dad had a very good friend from the Black Mountain days who was a barbecue wizard. His name was George Clayton. Mr. Clayton was a fellow miner who, as did most black miners, lived in "Colored Camp."

The following story might sound a bit startling to the modern ear. Remember as you read, it is Mr. Clayton himself, who tells this story.

Mr. Clayton was a jokester as well as an amazing barbecue man. He would frequently come up to Dad and say, "Carl, I don't know what I'm doing livin' in Colored Camp. I ain't no nigger, I'm an American Indian!" Dad would chuckle and say, "Well buddy, if you are, this camp here is full of Indians!" They would both get a big laugh out of this – and it became Mr. Clayton's routine line with Dad. He loved to pull this one out when he and Dad were with other friends.

George Clayton made his own barbecue sauce, as all true masters do. Many a man tried to beg, borrow, and steal his recipe, but to no avail. Mr. Clayton was often hired by clubs, outings, and Harlan's well-to-do to cook for their functions. He was very well known and highly respected.

A funny story involving Dad, George Clayton, and a barbecue grew out of one of Dad's fishing trips. He had been fishing with friends at Deep Cove and among his catch was a thirty-five pound channel catfish, which he caught on a trotline. Dad stopped by Mr. Clayton's to show him that fish and he said, "Carl, let me barbecue it. I'll make fish sandwiches out of it and sell 'em here in the camp. We'll split the money on it." Dad agreed, Mr. Clayton barbecued the fish, made and sold the fish sandwiches...and that was that!

Dad says:

We had us a big time over that one ever afterwards. Every time there was a bunch of us together I'd say, 'George, what happened to my cut from that catfish, buddy?'

George would say, 'Carl, I don't know nothin' about no catfish. I ain't seen no catfish.'

Then I'd tell 'em, 'Ol' George said he'd sell sandwiches from that big cat' I caught and we'd split the money. Well, he split alright. He split with ever' bit of that money!'

We'd all get such a big laugh out of that!

I chuckle to myself as I think this may have been a little bit of karma for Dad. Remember the story of the turkey shoot put together by Dad and Blab Davis? Mother was to receive the proceeds from the hotdog sales because she had made the chili for the 'dogs. Dad and Blab got a little busy with the beer and ended up just giving the hotdogs away. Mother got nothing for her time and effort – like Dad got nothing for the catfish sandwiches!

I got from Dad a love for cooking out. At least once a week in fair weather, you'll find me outside, grilling our dinner. On this same day last week, for example, I was barbecuing chicken. I always think of Dad when I grill; I think that is one reason I love it. Every time I coated that chicken with sauce, I'd think of Dad, and remember sitting by him long ago watching him do it. I hear him in my mind saying "You got to be patient, cook it slow, coat it in rounds, and let that sauce bake in good." Just like Dad, I make my own sauce using the secret recipe he gave me.

Note that I said, "the recipe he gave me" and not "Dad's recipe." It is not Dad's recipe. It is Mr. George Clayton's. That recipe of his, so coveted all over Harlan County, he gave to Dad. Dad gave it to me.

I love to sit on my deck and barbecue. I think of Dad, and my childhood. I think of Dad, and Mr. George Clayton, and stories of long ago.

And that sauce...Oh my!

CHAPTER 15

Was It Worth It?

I asked Dad why he thought miners mined. He said, "Well, they wasn't nothin' else in the area we could do, honey." I knew clearly what he meant by this. Unschooled labor living in an area controlled by a single industry has little choice but to work in that industry.

We measure things largely by two criteria. The first is, what did I get out of it? The second is, what did it cost me?

Dad got a lot out of mining. Mining gave him his *identity*, and that's about as much as one can get out of anything. As I said earlier, Dad would go on to *do* other careers, and do them well. But they would never define him. Mining did. Dad *was* a miner. It wasn't just something he did.

He got *meaning* from mining. All those pickets and skirmishes and struggles had a valiant meaning for Dad. They were to rectify a gross injustice – the mistreatment of the men who dug the coal, to abolish that old coal operator mentality and credo: "Kill a mule, buy a mule. Kill a man, hire a man." He and likeminded miners and organizers saw the struggle to unionize as not only looking out for themselves but for all future miners as well. (One thing that grieved Dad in his later years was seeing unions themselves abuse the power that had been so hard won by earlier generations. He despised the criminally convicted W. A. "Tony" Boyle,[86] the man who was soon to follow the revered John L. Lewis as president of the UMWA.)

Mining gave Dad a *brotherhood*. These men were in it together in the old days. It was not unlike the military in that sense. To call them "coworkers" wouldn't get it at all. They were way, way more than that to each other.

Mining gave Dad a *sense of success*. Dad grew up in the Depression, in very hard times. Working so hard to provide for his family in an extremely dangerous profession gave Dad a good feeling about himself as a man.

Lastly, and this one may be hard for us to understand, mining gave Dad *pleasure*. As strange as it might sound to our ears, Dad absolutely loved being underground. He loved the work, the arduous work of old-school mining. I think miners of that generation took a secret pride in knowing they were doing something that not every man could do. The claustrophobic conditions, the rigorous physical labor, the constant danger...it just wasn't something every man could handle. Forget whether one would *want* to or not, those miners knew they *could* do it, and that made them unique. Dad has talked to me many times about picking coal from his knees, then shoveling it sideways under a low roof onto a car or conveyor. As odd as it may seem to us, he was content, absolutely content there and yes, even happy.

Figure 43. Hand loading from knees in low top

Mining gave Dad a lot. It gave him things absolutely critical to a satisfying life, a sense of a well-lived life. However, these treasures Dad mined from mining came at a cost – and the price was high.

The physical repercussions from mining were severe – profound injuries, surgeries, black lung.

Relationally, Dad lost two brothers and many friends to mining. He never forgot the latter and he never got over the former.

Mining cost Dad psychologically. Wounds heal, but scars are with us for life. Mining scarred Dad. He bore it quietly and privately, but it was there. So many losses, so many sad and awful images in the mind.

Here is one final story from Dad to illustrate what I mean. It is a couple of years after the Battle of Evarts and many miners are barely subsisting. In fact, one slogan of the Harlan County miner then was "I'd rather strike and starve than work and starve." There was a roof fall in the 31 mine and one of the dirt-poor miners was killed. When his lunch kit was opened these were the contents – water and potato peels. Dad says:

> That's all he had. His wife later said her husband told her that morning to fry what was left of the potatoes for her and the kids for breakfast, and put the peelings in his lunch kit for his lunch, with some water.

Dad told me that story several times over my life and I don't ever recall him getting it out without tearing up.

The deepest, thickest scars, not surprisingly, are from the deaths of his brothers. He was shattered with grief by Chalk's death and riddled with guilt over Ed's.

Figure 44. Uncles Ed and Chalk, circa 1940

He knew, logically, that there was nothing more he could have done to prevent the wreck on Pine Mountain that horrible morning. But it didn't help much. As I tell my clients, a barren thought is rarely a match for an energized feeling. Dad *felt* responsible for Ed's death, no matter what his logical mind said to the contrary. More than anything else from his mining life, these two deaths scarred him.

If you asked Dad if it was worth the personal cost to him the answer was an unqualified yes. I do not mean, of course, the lives of his two brothers and more than a few mining friends over the years. Very little in life is worth so high a cost as that and mining certainly is not one of those few things. I am talking about the physical costs, the struggles, the pain, the personal sacrifice. Dad considered the price he paid to be a miner worth it. I know he did. I know because he told me so.

Coal-yard Facts

About 70% of the world's steel production relies on the use of coal to create its
product.

Conclusion

I hope the reader has enjoyed this journey through a time, and in some very real sense, a place now long gone. Virtually all of the mines and so many of the businesses, the buildings, even the roads are no longer to be found. More importantly, the majority of those people from the generation who lived this book are now gone. I return to what I said in the Introduction; rapidly, the time is approaching in which the only evidence these times even existed will reside in the stories handed down and written remembrances such as this.

Emerson says that all history is biography.[87] I said in the introduction that *Memory of a Miner* is an oral history, and this is certainly true. Following Emerson's observation, however, this is also a biography of sorts.

This book is the telling of one old-school miner's story. My sincere intent and hope is that this book honors Dad's life and memory, and tells his story well, for it is a story worth telling. In his early years, Dad was not an angel and he was not a demon. I've tried hard to present him as he was then – a man of many virtues and some ardent vices.

One of the characters – a writer – in *Don Quixote*, says to the outlandish knight-errant, "What I can tell

253

your grace is that [the writer's book] deals with truths. And they are truths so appealing and entertaining that no lies can equal them."[88] That is the experience I have hoped to create for the reader – the experience of being drawn into true stories "appealing and entertaining." If this goal has not been achieved, the error lies in my conveyance of them, and not in the stories themselves. Of that, I am certain.

I doubt a day goes by that I don't think of Dad, and miss him. I miss just knowing he's there. We live across from a beautiful lake and I rarely leave our subdivision but what I don't see Dad's face. He taught me to fish when I was a child in Harlan. We often fished together in the Poor Fork branch of the Cumberland River, just below Chappell's Dairy.

In my teen years, Dad, my brother-in-law, Buddy (Sandra's husband), and I spent many a day getting up way before dawn ("early of a-mornin'") and crappie fishing hard until dark. Buddy and I are never together long until we start telling fishing stories about Dad. (That would be a book in itself!) We know everybody's heard them; we know it full well. We aren't telling them to inform but to remember and relive by retelling. That very same reason is one of my chief motivations for writing this book.

My Christian faith tells me that Dad is not gone, just gone ahead. I take comfort in that.

Afterward

I have written this book for my own family. My sweet wife of thirty-seven years remembers Dad well, of course. Our son Jonathan, who is thirty-three, does as well. In fact, one of his greatest childhood memories is of a Christmas at Mother and Dad's. As always, there were twenty-five or so people there. Jonathan, about eight at the time, was sitting by Dad who was in rare form that night doing an impromptu comedy riff in Jonathan's ear concerning everything that was transpiring. He had Jonathan in stitches! This memory is indelibly inked in our son's mind.

Our daughter Jennifer, twenty-nine, remembers far less about "Papaw." She has heard all the stories of course, because I have shared them with her. I feel it is my duty and it is certainly my desire to pass them on. Another motivation for this book is that I want Jennifer to have a more permanent record of her grandfather's story.

I want Jennifer's husband, Adam, to get to know Dad better. We have shared the tales with him and this book will add to his knowledge and understanding of Dad. Although technically our son-in-law, Adam is like a second son to us.

Since I began this writing our family has grown by one. Susan and I are, for the first time, grandparents! Adam and Jennifer brought Caleb Michael Lett into this world 22 months ago. I want him to know his great-grandfather as well as possible. So, little man, this book is for you too!

I have written *Memory of a Miner* for my brother and sisters – Pat, Ronnie, and San. They knew Dad, the miner, and remember those years. This is especially true of Pat and Ronnie, the older two. Like me, my siblings have heard many of the stories I have put to pen their entire lives. Some of them they will no doubt remember firsthand for, unlike me, they were there. This is my gift to you, guys. I hope you enjoyed the read.

This book is for you, Mother. Though it is primarily Dad's story, it is certainly yours as well. You were there. You shared the joys and the pains, the highs and the lows, the good and the bad. Now that Dad is gone, no one but you knows what it was like to have lived it. I mean what I said of you in the chapter dedicated to your life – you are one strong woman!

Thanks for your help with this project, Mother. Without the several trips to Harlan County and those long talks around your kitchen table, there would be no book. And later, all those days spent on my deck where you filled in the details and the gaps make this story a much richer read. I will never forget the great times we had there! Thanks for the numerous readings of my notes and even the first draft of this book when no one but my immediate family and you even knew of its existence. There's no way I could have done it without you. More than any other person, I hope you enjoy the book and feel honored by it. You have given me your feedback on the project, and your words reinforce for me that I have succeeded in that intent. This pleases me immeasurably.

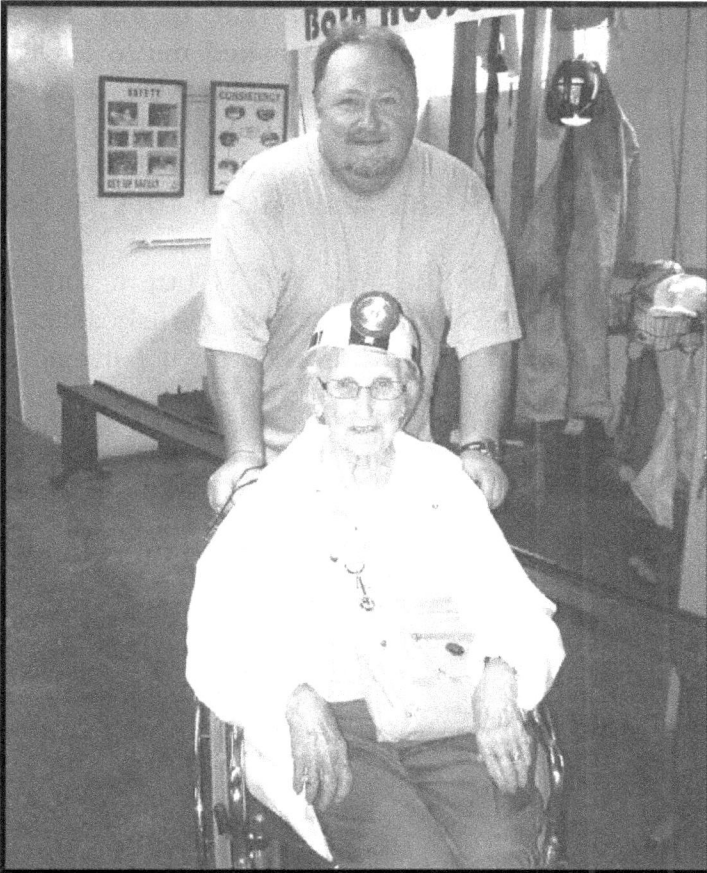

Figure 45. Mother and me in the Kentucky Coal Mining Museum in Benham. She got a kick out of donning the hard hat for this picture. The excellent museum is housed in what once was the company store.

Dad, ultimately this book is for you. It's been a long time coming. I know you would have a great crack about how long it has taken for me to finish it. I only wish you were here to give me one of your good-natured jibes for that!

I think you'd like the book, Dad. I have written other books and I gave each of them my best. But this one, for obvious reasons, is different. I've laughed and cried a hundred times while writing it. True to our talk, I've included nothing here that you asked me to leave out. I've even left out a good bit that you were okay with. Some of it just felt too personal and so, I left it at its source – with the conversations you, Mother, and I had around the kitchen table and on our trips to Harlan County.

Scripture tells us that our life is but a mist that appears for a little while and then vanishes.[89] I can therefore say with certainty that, even if I live to be a hundred, I'll see you soon, Dad.

Notes

Preface

[1] "Black Mountain" – Not to be confused with the Black Mountain which is just beyond Lynch, and hard by Appalachia, Virginia. The Black Mountain near Lynch is the highest natural point in the state of Kentucky. Both Black Mountains are in the Cumberland Range of the Southern Appalachian Mountains.

[2] "Kenvir" – A contraction of the names Kentucky and Virginia. The Virginia state line is just about five miles away and can be reached by crossing Black Mountain. Dad and his friends often went into Virginia to hunt and fish by traveling through the 31 mine.

Introduction

[3] "great stories happen" – Glass, Ira. "Our Friend David." Source: thisamericanlife.org/radio-archives/ episode _472/transcript.

Chapter 2 – A Brand Plucked from the Fire
[4] "plucked from the fire" – a quotation from Zechariah 3:2.

Chapter 3 – The Boy is Key to the Man
[5] "Dad grew up the youngest" – The children, in order, were Lawrence, Emma, Ervin, Ed, Charles ("Chalk"), Carl, and Helen Charlene. As you read on in this chapter, you will discover why I call Dad the youngest.

[6] "The powerlessness Dad felt" – An ongoing absence or insufficiency of power typically leads to frustration. Very often, that frustration results in the development of anger as an habitual coping mechanism. It certainly did in the case of Dad.

[7] "wild behavior of hillbillies" – The New York Times, 18 May, 1922.

[8] "at the Hignite mine" – Dad's recall is uncertain here. This could have either been the Hignite Coal Company in Middlesboro or the one just a few miles away in Chenoa. Both were in Bell County.

[9] "Cook & Sharpe Mining Company" – Here is another of those spelling anomalies. Within the company name, sometimes the latter man's name is "Sharpe," at other times, "Sharp."

[10] "Typhoid fever" – An often deadly disease in this time, and common enough in mining camps. In fact, it was often referred to as "camp fever." Typhoid fever is a bacterial-based (salmonella typhi) illness which, in the Southern Appalachia of the day, was usually due to

contaminated food and/or water sources. Google "Typhoid Mary" for a compelling story.

[11] "Black Mountain mine" – A huge operation. At its peak, the mines had just under 850 employees. Source: coaleducation.org/coalhistory/coaltowns/coalcamps/ harlan_county_coal_camps.htm.

Chapter 4 – Carl and Della
[12] "Chevrolet Mine" – This was likely the Blue Diamond Coal Company mine in Chevrolet.

[13] "clubhouse in Coxton" – All that remains today are portions of the foundation and sections of the surrounding stone wall.

[14] "amateur baseball team" – Coxton's baseball field, which I can remember many years later from my childhood, is gone. An outdoor basketball court and park now occupy that property.

[15] "at the Brookside Mine" – Prior to the "new road" from Harlan to Evarts, the road crossed the tracks right in front of the Brookside company store.

Chapter 5 – Struggle and Sacrifice
[16] "the first train of coal" – Kentucky's Eastern Coal Field sits in portions of 37 counties and occupies some 10,500 square miles. It is estimated that the amount of coal originally in those deposits amounts to 105 billion tons, of which less than 20% has been extracted. Source: http://kycoal.homestead.com/kycoalmining history.html. (Per Jim Wallace, a native of Black Mountain I spoke with, as of this writing only Brookside

and Highsplint ship their coal by rail. All others truck their coal to Virginia, where it is then sent by train to its destination.)

[17] "The profits were massive" – Even as late as 1975, this trend continued. Note the following statistics from that year:
cost of living – up 7%
miners' wages – up 4%
coal company profits – up 170%.
Source: Kopple, Barbara, producer and director. Harlan County, USA. Cabin Creek Films, 1976.

[18] "Snuff Street" – As a point of trivial interest, this is not the road's actual name (which is Highway 38). The locals called it "Snuff Street" because the houses that lined it were so close to the sidewalk that residents could sit on the front porch and spit their snuff juice onto the sidewalk. Those really adept at the art could spit all the way to the street – hence, Snuff Street.

[19] "New York (Kentucky King)" – "The Kentucky Miners Struggle." American Civil Liberties Union, May, 1932, 4. As found at debs.indstate.edu/a505k4_1932.pdf.

[20] "Battle of Evarts" – For the backdrop to the Battle of Evarts, and events that led up to it, see: Passos, John Dos. "Harlan: Working under the Gun." The New Republic, 2 Dec, 1931; Titler, George J. Hell in Harlan, chapter 4; and "The Kentucky Miners Struggle." American Civil Liberties Union, May, 1932.

21 "reduction was enacted" – Hevener, John W. <u>Which Side are You On?: The Harlan County Coal Miners, 1931-39</u>, 33.

22 "the Kaiser" – Titler, <u>Hell in Harlan</u>, 25.

23 "Benham and Lynch" – Source for number of employees: coaleducation.org/coalhistory/coaltownscoal camps/harlan_county_coal_camps.htm.

24 "Feudal Lords of Harlan" – Titler, <u>Hell in Harlan</u>, 103.

25 "treatment of him" – <u>Knoxville News Sentinel</u>, as quoted in McEntee, Gerald and Lee Saunders. <u>The Main Street Moment</u>, 48.

26 "must be abolished" – I have compiled this list from a number of sources. The source for the actual report from which they are taken is: U.S. Congress. House. From the Report of the Denhardt Commission. Congressional Record, 74th Cong., 1st sess. (1935), vol. 79, 8987-8988.

27 "to aid the coal operators" - Louisville "Courier-Journal," March 27, 1932, as quoted in Hevener, <u>Which Side Are You On?</u>, 16.

28 "in Harlan County" – Report of the Hays-Bablitz Commission, quoted in United Mine Workers Journal, Jan 15, 1932, 6, as quoted in Hevener, <u>Which Side Are You On?</u>, 16.

29 "hungry children here" – Source: groups.google.com/ forum/#!topic/mormons-only-speak-out/eZJLMWjqC0I.

[30] *"Lay the Lily Low"* – Source: oocities.org/folkfred/whichsid.html.

[31] "from legitimate county funds" - Titler, <u>Hell in Harlan</u>, 106.

[32] "paid by the coal operators" – Scott, Shaunna L. <u>Two Sides to Everything: The Cultural Construction of Class Consciousness in Harlan County, Kentucky</u>, 28.

[33] "guard at Three Point" – Portelli, Alessandro. <u>They Say in Harlan County: An Oral History</u>, 187.

[34] "in perfect Chicago style" – Dos Passos, John. "Harlan: Working Under the Gun," 3. <u>The New Republic</u>, 2 December 1931, as found at newdeal.feri.org/voices/voce04.htm.

[35] "election officials of fraud" – Hevener, <u>Which Side Are You On?</u>, 16.

[36] "from the blast site" – Klotter, James A. <u>Kentucky: Portrait in Paradox, 1900-1950</u>, 142-143.

[37] "from Harlan County government" – Scott, <u>Two Sides to Everything</u>, 28.

[38] "own dairy farm" – Source: archiver.rootsweb.ancestry.com/th/read/ky-coalminers/2006-/1137089237.

[39] "coal operations in the county" – Hevener, <u>Which Side Are You On?</u>, 17-18.

[40] "A scab has not" – This assessment of a "scab" is generally attributed to Jack London, although there is credible disagreement about this. The full diatribe reads as follows:

After God had finished the rattlesnake, the toad, the vampire, He had some awful substance left with which He made a scab. A scab is a two-legged animal with a cork-screw soul, a water-logged brain, a combination backbone of jelly and glue. Where others have hearts, he carries a tumor of rotten principles. When a scab comes down the street, men turn their backs and angels weep in heaven, and the Devil shuts the gates of Hell to keep him out.

No man has a right to scab so long as there is a pool of water to drown his carcass in, or a rope long enough to hang his body with. Judas Iscariot was a gentleman compared with a scab. For betraying his master, he had character enough to hang himself. A scab has not. Esau sold his birth-right for a mess of pottage. Judas Iscariot sold his Savior for thirty pieces of silver. Benedict Arnold sold his country for a promise of a commission in the British Army. The modern strikebreaker sells his birthright, his country, his wife, his children and his fellow men for an unfulfilled promise from his employer, trust or corporation.

Esau was a traitor to himself: Judas Iscariot was a traitor to his God; Benedict Arnold was a traitor to his country; a strikebreaker is a traitor to his God, his country, his wife, his family and his class.

[41] "When we went to Three Point" - Not to be confused with the Three Point Coal Company which operated earlier (1923-1930), in nearby Lenarue. The Three Point mine under discussion was in operation 1931-1957. Source: coaleducation.org/coalhistory/coaltowns/coal camps/harlan_county_coal_camps.htm.

Chapter 6 – In Coal Blood

[42] "Happy Chandler" – Chandler would resign his gubernatorial position in October of 1939, so that the newly elevated Governor, Keen Johnson, could appoint him to the U. S. Senate. The seat opened as the result of the death of Kentucky's Senator M. M. Logan.

[43] "to help them" – Source: progressivehistorians.com /2008/05/which-side-are-you-on.html.

[44] "of integrity will not touch" – Perhaps surprisingly, the most horrific and unconscionable mining conflict in the U. S. occurred not in West Virginia, Kentucky, or Pennsylvania but in Colorado. In September of 1913, 1200 miners went on strike against Colorado mine owners for what could be summed as barbaric labor practices. All miners and families were immediately evicted from the company housing. Anticipating this, the UMWA had leased land in Ludlow and erected a tent community for the miners and their families.

The companies used their own "gun thugs" and even hired the Baldwin–Felts Detective Agency – famous as aggressive strike breakers – to serve as "mine guards." (Among their tactics was harassing the tent community and to do random drive by shootings into tents indiscriminately. Miners and their family members were wounded and killed in these assaults. To try and improve their safety, miners would dig shallow pits in the ground of their tents for their families to lay in during assaults.)

In October 28, 1913, Governor Ammons called in the Colorado National Guard who immediately made it clear they sided with the owner/operators. On April 20, 1914 tensions came to a head. Miners saw the Colorado National Guard and the "mine guards" hired by the coal companies establishing machine gun placements on the high ground overlooking the tent community. Firing erupted from both parties. The miners had nothing but small firearms. Either from incoming fire or incendiary devices, the tent village was in flames by the evening. (The conflict had gone on for hours.) Those who could fled the village and the companies' troops then advanced and looted what was left to be had. The community burned to the ground.

When the carnage ended four company men had been killed. Some twenty-plus residents of the tent village had died. That number includes two women and eleven children. The camp leader, a brave Greek immigrant and coal miner named Louis Tikas, was captured by the companies' militia and taken away. He was found some time after the battle subsided. He had been shot dead...in the back.

The largest of the Colorado coal companies and the chief protagonist in the oppression of the miners and their families was the Colorado Fuel and Iron Company. The principal owner of that mine was John D. Rockefeller, Jr. This historic tragedy is known worldwide as the Ludlow Massacre.

[45] "going to Mary Helen" – There had been picketing the day before (April 1, 1942) at Mary Helen and the nearby

R. C. Tway mine. Although some men from Black Mountain had been present at these pickets, Dad, his brothers, and closest friends had not. The friction at Mary Helen was especially strident that day. In a shootout with a miner one mine guard had been killed.

[46] "a good many of us" – According to the 4/21/41 edition of the Harlan Daily Enterprise, there were some 50 cars of miners at the Mary Helen and Crummies Creek pickets that day. This would likely equate to about 250 men. This is nearly 90% less than the inflated 2,000 men, reported by the highly prejudiced Chicago Tribune (4/3/41).

[47] "Browning Automatic Rifle" – The B.A.R. seems to have been a favorite weapon of the "deputies" hired by the operators. As noted in the text, this was a military weapon akin to the machine gun.

[48] "that had been killed" – The Harlan Daily Enterprise (4/21/41) reported that Virgil Hampton died in the Harlan Hospital shortly after being taken there. If so his body was transported rapidly to the morgue because Dad clearly remembered his body being in the room with Chalk and Ed Tye.

[49] "just left Lawrence's house" – The house Uncle Lawrence and his family lived in (Coxton) still stands as of this writing and is occupied.

[50] "cigarettes and his union card" - Dad gave these two items to me many years ago. Once, while talking with Dad for this book, he mentioned that he would like to give Chalk's cigarettes and his union card to Chalk's

son Bobby, now deceased. I returned them to Dad for that purpose. I am not sure as to whether he got those possessions to Bobby or not.

51 "Sally Howard's restaurant" – for more on this colorful character and miner's friend, see Hell in Harlan, Chapter 20.

52 "just mowed the men down" – Portelli, They Say in Harlan County, 240. By permission of Oxford University Press, USA.

53 "We died just like ducks" – Portelli, They Say in Harlan County, 231-232. By permission of Oxford University Press, USA.

54 "mob and labor goons" - Chicago Tribune, 2 April, 1941 and 7 February, 1949, respectively.

Chapter 7 – 31 Camp
55 "including one of the sons" – On this particular delivery by Mom the story is this. Dora Montgomery had gone into labor and the camp doctor had been sent for. Mom was on hand with Mrs. Montgomery. The baby came before the doctor arrived and Mom, as she had done with numerous other women, delivered him.

56 "They were a community" – The very word community means "to have in common." In the coal camps all the men had related jobs and struggles, the wives had related responsibilities and worries, and the children had related peers. In short, the families all shared nearly identical lifestyles. Any group of people would be

hard pressed to have more "in common" than did those within a coal camp.

57 "to Punkin Center" – this is the historic and familiar name to the community above 31 Camp, along the main road (state road 215). The postal name is Dizney, but it was rarely called this by locals. Dizney seems to be the preferred name today.

58 "what he died of" – According to the death certificate, Grandpa Ruth died of moist gangrene and diabetes.

59 "if you'd had your arm cut off" – Curiously, Dad often had phantom pain in his left thumb, but never once in the area of the missing little finger.

60 "man trip" – a string of specially designed low-roofed cars pulled by a motor car. The man trip delivered the miners into the mine at the beginning of a shift and out of it at the end.

61 "you'ns didn't say nothin'" – "You'ns" is a common expression heard in rural areas of Southern Appalachia. It is a contraction of the Scottish "you ones."

62 "his carbide light" – Carbide lights were used in Black Mountain until about 1939-40. After that, a battery powered model was used. Source: kenvir.fateback.com /Kelly-martin.html.

63 "when it came to jitterbugging" – The origin of this term is one of those fun facts. The true name of this dance is "swing." Some observer watching swing dancers in action commented that they looked like

"jitterbugs." The name caught on and stuck to describe the style of dance itself.

[64] "reach for his hardware" – Supina, Phillip D. "Herndon J Evans and the Harlan County Coal Strike." The Filson Club History Quarterly, vol. 56, p. 316, July 1982. As found at eris.uky.edu/catalog/xt7zcr5n9g1t_ 34_76.

[65] "dark and bloody ground" – Klotter, James. "Feuds in Appalachia: An Overview." The Filson Club History Quarterly, vol. 56, p. 291, July 1982. As found at eris.uky.edu/catalog/xt7zcr5n9g1t_34_51.

[66] "classic nature/nurture dynamic" – Personality is formed by the interplay of two basic factors: nature (genetic predispositions) and nurture (developmental experiences). In Dad's case, this includes his Irish temperament and ethos (nature) and his experiences of being the youngest brother and, like his siblings, the recipient of severe discipline from his father (nurture).

Chapter 8 – The War Years
[67] "industry runs on coal" – Demand and mechanization have severely impacted Kentucky's coal industry. During the 1950s more than 12,000 men mined in Harlan County. By the late 1980s, that number had dropped to less than 3,500. "Coal War Scars Have Grown Over," Chicago Tribune, September 18, 1988.

[68] "came to Harlan County" - Perhaps surprisingly, Harlan County was a real melting pot of ethnic groups. Eastern and Western Europe were especially well represented.

[69] "to be unconstitutional" – Source: sherwoodtenn.com /lynch/lynch_kentucky.htm.

[70] "to the company store" – The song is, of course, *Sixteen Tons*. It was first recorded by Merle Travis in 1946. The song became a world-wide hit in 1955, when Tennessee Ernie Ford recorded it.

[71] "right now but robbin' work" – There can be more coal left in the pillars than was mined from the sections. Today "robbing" is called retreat mining.

[72] "outside the camps" – Coal camps were practically a dominion unto themselves (or more accurately, unto the coal companies that owned them). These were areas on American soil which: were not incorporated, had no elections or elected officials, stamped their own currency (scrip), basically had their own police force ("deputies"), controlled completely the commerce within their confines, and determined independently who could and could not live within them.

Chapter 10 – An Iron-Strong Woman

[73] "move from Evarts" – Mom and her three daughters moved to East Bernstadt for 6-7 months. From there they moved back to Evarts, as stated. Less than a year later, at the persistent pleas of Mom's sister Cordia (Cordelia), they move to Corbin. (Aunt Cordia lived there.) They lived in Corbin less than a year when they, missing Evarts, decided to move back home. Mom bought a house on Evart's hill, up behind the Baptist church on Highway 38. Mother had started the 8th grade in Corbin but they were back in Evarts in time for her to finish the school year there.

[74] "win a medal" – Titler, <u>Hell in Harlan</u>, 170.

[75] "the cruellest month" – Eliot, T. S. <u>The Waste Land</u>, I, 1.

[76] "December takes that claim" – Ironically, the horrible Yancey mine disaster of 1932, in Harlan County, also occurred in December (Friday, 12/9/1932). Winter was the worst time of year for coal dust-related explosions. The dry air made it more likely for the dust to suspend in the air, where the tiniest of sparks could ignite it, resulting in violent explosions. Twenty-three miners died in the Yancey (Yancy) disaster.

[77] "made even crueler" – Another cruelty in mining accidents was the fact that a single family would often lose several members. This was because sons were likely to follow fathers into mining and brothers follow brothers. For example, six Massengill brothers died in the Yancey disaster mentioned above.

There was a time when a disaster at Black Mountain could have taken out Grandpa and four of his boys. For a period he, Lawrence, Ed, Chalk, and Dad all worked at the mine together.

[78] "methane gas" – Coal is a fossil fuel. This means it results from the decomposition of organic material. When organic matter decomposes methane gas is created. When coal is mined, the highly explosive methane gas releases into the air. (Which is why the miners often called it "seeping gas.") Mine safety, including that of methane gas, often woefully lacking or even absent in the past, is seriously monitored in most mines today.

[79] "coal dust explosion" – Mining results in coal dust being suspended in the mine's air. Coal dust is explosive. The pulverized coal mined today for coal-burning power plants generates the most dust of all. The combination of a high concentration of coal dust, oxygen and an igniter (fire, spark, etc.) makes for hazardous work! Most of today's mines do a good job of controlling coal dust emissions in the mine. (To see a controlled explosion of coal dust follow this link: youtube/watch?v=8p9HxH3Iht8. Pay special attention to the upper half of the video, which shows an unsuppressed dust explosion as would have occurred in the old days. Note especially the eerie backdraft after the explosion.).

[80] "black damp" – Black damp is a toxic mixture of carbon dioxide (coal absorbs oxygen and gives off carbon dioxide), water vapor, and nitrogen. Basically, it is air deprived of sufficient oxygen and thus, is an asphyxiant. Black damp typically follows a mine explosion and is therefore called "after damp" often. Barring rapid rescue efforts, for miners trapped with black damp for air, death is certain.

On May 19,1902, the worst mining disaster in Tennessee history occurred at the Coal Creek Coal Company's Fraterville (near Lake City) mine. The explosion (likely Methane gas) and subsequent black damp killed 216 miners. Several of the miners who died from black damp wrote letters to their family before succumbing to the poisonous air. Jacob Vowell wrote the following heartbreaking last words to his wife:

Ellen, darling Good Bye for us both. Elbert
said the Lord had saved him. We are all

praying for air to support us but it is getting so bad without any air.

Ellen, I want you to live right and come to heaven. Raise the children the best you can. Good Bye Ellen Good Bye Lily Good Bye Jimmie Good Bye Horace. Is 25 minutes after Two. There is a few of us are alive yet. JAKE & ELBERT.

Oh God for one more breath. Ellen, remember me as long as you live.

Good Bye Darling

Source: usmra.com/repository/category/mine_rescue/ coal_history.ppt.

[81] "than men at work" – Source: Bellcountypublic libraries.org/crm/ky/ bell/miller3.html.

Chapter 11- The Good Times

[82] "wettest dry county" – Actually, Harlan was a "moist" county. Cumberland sold alcohol legally but Harlan and Evarts, for example, could not. All three are in Harlan County.

[83] "moonshine whiskey" – Ah yes, Appalachia's famous moonshine. A few points of interest about the elixir:

The word "whiskey" is derived from the Gaelic (Scot/Irish) term "uisce beatha" – pronounced "ishka baha." The term means "water of life," in Gaelic. The full term was shortened to just "uisce" (pronounced "ishka"), which the early American settlers pronounced as "whiskey." The Irish have been distilling whiskey since the sixth century.

Moonshine gets its name from the working habits of the 'shiners themselves. Moonshiners learned quickly that it was better to work at night, under the light (shine) of the moon so government agents couldn't see the smoke from the fire under their stills. (It didn't take mountain men long to learn that there was a lot more money to be made from a bushel of corn sold as moonshine than a bushel of corn sold as produce!)

Moonshine stills are so called because of the large (often copper) pot which is at the center of the distilling apparatus. That pot is called the "still pot."

Why is moonshine clear? For obvious reasons, 'shiners are unable (nor do they desire) to barrel-age their whiskey. This barrel aging, using charred oak barrels, is what gives aged whiskey its amber hue. Because 'shine is clear ("white") and because it kicks like a mule, it came to be called "white lightening."

The most famous of all of Appalachia's moonshiners, Marvin "Popcorn" Sutton, died March 16, 2009.

[84] "it is too bad" – Scott, Two Sides to Everything, 28.

[85] "but a hole" – The population of Harlan County was approximately 80,000 in the 1950s. In 2012, according to the Federal Census, the population had dropped to 28,543.

According to the U. S. Federal Reserve, the unemployment rate for Harlan County was 14.6% in July, 2012. This is a 13 year high, and is near double the current national unemployment rate (of 7.6%). Source: tradingeconomics.com/united-states/unemploy ment-rate-in-harlan-county-ky-percent-m-nsa-fed-data. html.

Chapter 15 – Was It Worth It?

[86] "W. A. 'Tony' Boyle" – On December 31, 1969, a three-man hit team allegedly hired by Boyle killed Joseph "Jock" Yablonski, his wife, and their 25-year-old daughter while they were asleep at home. Yablonski had been Boyle's opponent in the 1969 election for the presidency of the UMWA. Boyle reportedly paid the killers $20,000, which he had embezzled from union funds.

Boyle had won the 1969 election, which was later deemed in court to have been rigged. A federal judge overturned the election results and a new election was ordered. Arnold Miller defeated Boyle in the new election of December, 1972. This time, the election process was overseen by the U. S. Department of Labor.

In 1973, Boyle was sentenced to three years for embezzling union funds. In 1978, he was convicted of the Yablonski murders and given a life sentence. W. A. 'Tony' Boyle died in 1985.

Conclusion

[87] "all history is biography" – Emerson's exact phrase is: "there is properly no history; only biography." Emerson, Ralph Waldo, History, in Essays – First Series, 3.

[88] "no lies can equal them" – The character speaking is Ginés de Pasamonte. Don Quixote 1, XXII, 169.

Afterward

[89] "and then vanishes" – James 4:14.

Bibliography

"1 Dead, 4 Wounded in Kentucky Feud: Rival Witnesses at a Murder Trial Open Fire on Each Other in Court House. " The New York Times, 18 May, 1922.

archiver.rootsweb.ancestry.com/th/read/ky-coalminers /2006-01/1137089237.

bellcountypubliclibraries.org/crm/ky/bell/miller3.html.

Biblical Citations: Zechariah 3:2, James 4:14.

Chicago Tribune, 2 April, 1941.

_____. 3 April, 1941.

_____. 7 February, 1949.

coaleducation.org/coalhistory/coaltowns/coalcamps/ha rlan_county_coal_camps.htm.

"Coal War Scars Have Grown Over." Chicago Tribune, 18 September, 1988.

De Cervantes, Miguel. Don Quixote, trans Edith Grossman. Translation copyright 2003, Edith Grossman. New York: HarperCollins, 2005.

Dos Passos, John. "Harlan: Working Under the Gun." The New Republic, 2 December, 1931, 3, as found at http://newdeal.feri.org/voices/voce04.htm.

Eliot, T. S. The Waste Land, Kindle edition.

Emerson, Ralph Waldo. History. In Essays – First Series, Kindle edition.

Glass, Ira. "Our Friend David." At thisamericanlife. org/radio-archives/episode_472 /transcript.

Hevener, John W. Which Side Are You On?: The Harlan County Coal Miners, 1931-1939. University of Illinois, 1978.

Harlan Daily Enterprise, 21 April, 1941.

indstate.edu/a505k4_1932.pdf.

kenvir.fateback.com/Kelly-martin.html.

Klotter, James. Feuds in Appalachia: An Overview. The Filson Club History Quarterly, vol. 56, July 1982. As found at eris.uky.edu/catalog/xt7zcr5n9g1t_34_51.

_____. Kentucky: Portrait in Paradox, 1900-1950. Lexington: Kentucky Historical Society. 142-3.

Knoxville News Sentinel, 1931, as quoted in The Main Street Moment, p. 48.

Kopple, Barbara, producer and director. Harlan County, USA. Cabin Creek Films, 1976.

kycoal.homestead.com/kycoalmininghistory.html.

Louisville Courier-Journal, 27 March, 1932.

McEntee, Gerald and Lee Saunders. The Main Street Moment: Fighting Back to Save the American Dream. New York: Nation Books, 2012.

newdeal.feri.org/voices/voce04.htm.

oocities.org/folkfred/whichsid.html.

Portelli, Alessandro. They Say in Harlan County: An Oral History. New York: Oxford University Press, 2011.

progressivehistorians.com/2008/05/which-side-are-you-on.html.

Scott, Shaunna L. "Two Sides to Everything: The Cultural Construction of Class Consciousness in Harlan County, Kentucky." PhD diss., State University of New York, 1995.

sherwoodtenn.com/lynch/lynch_kentucky.htm.

Supina, Phillip D. "Herndon J Evans and the Harlan County Coal Strike." The Filson Club History Quarterly, vol. 56, July 1982. As found at eris.uky.edu/catalog/xt7zcr5n9g1t_34_76.

"The Kentucky Miners Struggle." American Civil Liberties Union, May, 1932.

"They Don't Teach This In American History,,,,,Lest We Forget." At groups.google.com/forum/#!topic/mormons-only-speak-out/eZJLMWjqCOI.

Titler, George J. Hell in Harlan. By the author, 1972.

tradingeconomics.com/united-states/unemployment-rate-in-harlan-county-ky-percent-m-nsa-fed-data.html.

U.S. Congress. House. From the Report of the Denhardt Commission. Congressional Record, 74th Cong., 1st sess. (1935), vol. 79, 8987-8988.

usmra.com/repository/category/mine_rescue/coal_history.ppt.

youtube/watch?v=8p9HxH3Iht8.

Index

72, 263
Feudal system, 73
Financial giants, 61
Fire, 13, 15, 16, 23, 49,
    68, 71, 201, 202, 212,
    213, 215, 260, 267,
    274, 276
First Reader, 172, 173
Fish, 35, 135, 148, 213,
    214, 245, 254, 259
Fishin', 115, 132
Fishing, 35, 116, 117,
    134, 148, 171, 213,
    245, 254
Floatin' power, 154
Florida, 148
Floyd, Charles Arthur
    "Pretty Boy," 130
Floyd, K. P., 129, 130,
    230
Flying Miner of Kenvir,
    126
Flying squadrons, 74
Ford, Henry, 61
Fordson Coal Co., 61
Forrest, Jimmy, 137
Fraterville mine, 275
Fraud, 77, 78, 264
Friday's Radio Shop,
    101
Frieda, 208, 209
Froze stiff, 238
Fuller Furniture Store,
    45
Funeral, 68, 104, 117,
    192, 239

G

Gambling, 116, 117, 145
Gary, IN, 70
Gas station, 70, 225
Glass, Ira, 5
Gon, 93, 94, 95, 119,
    120, 120f
Good Samaritan, 118,
    142, 193
Goodlin, Oscar, 98, 102
Gospel of John, 105
Governor Ammons, 267
Grainger County, TN, 11
Grapefruit, 37
Grave, 75f, 106f, 142,
    188, 233, 240f
Graveyard, 40, 64
Great Depression, 34,
    35, 174, 176, 248
Great Heart Coal, 120,
    120f
Grenades, 85
Greyhound Bus, 148
Ground water, 63
Gubernatorial vote, 77
Gun thugs, 64, 65, 66,
    70, 79, 80, 81, 82, 83,
    85, 103, 187, 199,
    266
Gunmen, 71, 73

H

Halloween, 48
Ham bone, 32
Hampton, Betsy, 48
Hampton, Lionel, 137
Hampton, Virgil, 98,
    102, 268
Hardware, 96, 140, 271

Q

R

S

T

W

Y

We hope reading *Memory of a Miner* has brought you some laughter, some knowledge, and perhaps even a tear or two. And if mining has been a part of your family heritage, maybe even a few memories of your own have been rekindled.

It is our sincere wish that you enjoyed the read as much as we have enjoyed sharing it with you!

We invite you to visit us at:

memoryofaminer.com

facebook.com/memoryofaminer

✂ Give the gift of *Memory of a Miner*
to family and friends

YES, please send me _____ copies of *Memory of a Miner*
at $19.95 each (TN residents add $1.95 sales tax per book).
Canadian orders must be accompanied by postal money
order in U.S. funds and allow 15 days for delivery.
  Shipping for all orders: $5 for first book, $2 each additional book

• My check or money order for $_____ is enclosed **OR**
• Please charge my: ___Visa ___MasterCard ___Am Ex

Name on card: _____
Billing address: _____

_____
Card #:_____
Exp date: _____ 3 or 4 digit security code:_____
Phone: _____
Signature: _____

Shipping address, if different from above:
Name: _____
Shipping address: _____

_____

Make check payable and return to:
Growth Resources
PO Box 23751
Knoxville, TN 37933

OR Fax this form to: **1-888-847-9303**
OR Order online at: **memoryofaminer.com**

www.ingramcontent.com/pod-product-compliance
Lightning Source LLC
Chambersburg PA
CBHW060249100426
42742CB00011B/1687